Timeless Top 10 Travel Guides

Paris

Paris' Top 10 Hotel Districts, Shopping and Dining, Museums, Activities, Historical Sights, Nightlife, Top Things to do Off the Beaten Path, and Much More!

By Tess Downey

Disclaimer and Legal Notice

This product is not legal, medical, or accounting advice and should not be interpreted in that manner. You need to do your own due-diligence to determine if the content of this product is right for you. While every attempt has been made to verify the information shared in this publication, neither the author, neither publisher, nor the affiliates assume any responsibility for errors, omissions or contrary interpretation of the subject matter herein. Any perceived slights to any specific person(s) or organization(s) are purely unintentional.

We have no control over the nature, content and availability of the web sites listed in this book. The inclusion of any web site links does not necessarily imply a recommendation or endorse the views expressed within them. We take no responsibility for, and will not be liable for, the websites being temporarily unavailable or being removed from the internet.

The accuracy and completeness of information provided herein and opinions stated herein are not guaranteed or warranted to produce any particular results, and the advice and strategies, contained herein may not be suitable for every individual. Neither the author nor the publisher shall be liable for any loss incurred as a consequence of the use and application, directly or indirectly, of any information presented in this work. This publication is designed to provide information in regard to the subject matter covered. Neither the author nor the publisher assume any responsibility for any errors or omissions, nor do they represent or warrant that the ideas, information, actions, plans, suggestions contained in this book is in all cases accurate. It is the reader's responsibility to find advice before putting anything written in this book into practice. The information in this book is not intended to serve as legal, medical, or accounting advice.

Foreword

Paris is the French capital city and it is one of Europe's flagship cities in both culture and business. No one will ever get enough of this historical paradise, locals and tourists alike, because Paris has already proven so much over the years and it stood the test of time. It will continue to flourish as one of the greatest cities that this world or even this universe has to offer for centuries!

Immerse yourself in the city's past through its different arts and culture festivals, historical monuments, and delicate dishes; experience what Paris can offer today through its various tourist destinations, vibrant nightlife and amazing people; prepare yourself to be a part of its future as it becomes one of the key cities that is going to shape the world we live in.

Embark on a fun-filled journey that will last you a lifetime, own every second that Paris could offer and learn why this city is known as "the city of light and the city of love" just like many Europeans and lovers that came before you.

Table of Contents

Paris 1

Introduction 1

Chapter One: Paris Overview 5

Paris in Focus 6

A Brief History of Paris 8

Paris' Language, People and Culture 11

Chapter Two: Travel Essentials 15

Visa and Passport Requirements 16

Chapter Three: Getting In and Around Paris 31

Chapter Four: Hotels and Accommodations 39

1. **Le Marais District** 41
2. **St. Germain - des - Pres District** 43
3. **Montmartre District** 45
4. **9th District** 47
5. **Ile Saint - Louis District** 49
6. **Belleville District** 51
7. **Opera District** 53

8. Champs Elysees 55

9. Gare de Lyon District 57

10. Wagram Monceau 59

Chapter Five: Fine Dining 61

1. 11th Arrondissement 62

2. 10th Arrondissement 64

3. 8th Arrondissement 66

4. 9th Arrondissement 68

5. 2nd Arrondissement 70

6. 6th Arrondissement 72

7. 3rd Arrondissement 74

8. 1st Arrondissement 76

9. 18th Arrondissement 77

10. 4th Arrondissement 79

Chapter Six: Shopping in Paris 81

1. Avenue des Champs Elysees 82

2. Rue de Rennes 85

3. Haussmann – Opera 87

4. Rue de Rivoli - Le Marais 89

5. Rue des Martyrs 91

6. Rue Saint-Honoré 93

7. Montmartre District 95

8. Rue de Passy 97

9. Avenue des Ternes 99

10. Quartier Beaubourg et Les Halles 101

Chapter Seven: Tourist Spots in Paris 105

1. The Eiffel Tower (La Tour Eiffel) 106

2. Louvre Museum and Pyramid 109

3. Notre Dame Cathedral (Notre Dame de Paris) 112

4. Seine River 115

5. Sacre Coeur Basilica 118

6. Château de Versailles (Palace of Versailles) 121

7. Pantheon 124

8. L'Hotel National des Invalides 127

9. Élysée Palace 130

10. Arc de Triomphe 133

Chapter Eight: Interacting with Paris 137

2. Moulin Rouge Theater 141

3. Musée d'Art moderne de la Ville de Paris 143

4. Jardin des Tuileries 145

5. Maison européenne de la photographie 147

6. Centre de Création Artistique 150

7. Grand Musée du Parfum 152

8. Parc zoologique de Thoiry 155

9. Cité de l'Architecture & du Patrimoine 157

10. Jardin du Luxembourg 159

Chapter Nine: Nightlife in Paris 163

1. Bastille 164

2. Oberkampf 166

3. Ménilmontant and Gambetta 168

4. The Marais 170

5. Belleville 172

6. Champs-Elysées 174

7. Montmartre and Pigalle 176

8. Grands Boulevards and Sentier 178

9. St – Germain – des – Prés 180

10. Place Vendome - Faubourg St-Honoré 182

Chapter Ten: Off - Beaten Path in Paris 185

1. Gaîté Lyrique 186

2. La Pagode 188

3. Le Ballon de Paris 190

4. Le Carreau du Temple 192

5. Musée Rodin 194

6. Fondation Louis Vuitton 196

7. Saint – Chapelle 198

8. Musée Eugène Delacroix 200

9. Passage Vivienne 202

10. Cimetière du Père Lachaise 204

Quick Travel Guide 207

1. Paris Quick Facts 208
2. Transportation 209
3. Travel Essentials 209

Paris Highlights 211

PHOTO REFERENCES 217

REFERENCES 229

Introduction

If you think about it, Paris really needs no introduction, but I wanted to emphasize why this great city continues to be one of the best cities in the world - perhaps one that I hope everyone can visit in their lifetime. It's not just because of its history or glamorous lifestyle, not even because of its world - renowned tourist spots but mainly because of its people; how the Parisians have survived and continued to be united in times of trouble, and how each one of them strived to keep their beautiful city intact for future generations.

This is the city where art meets culture, and where culture meets life! Only in Paris can you see people, particularly tourists, appreciating art even if they really don't care about it before; whether it is paintings, architecture, fashion or the people's way of life in general. Isn't that weird? The city will definitely bring out the artistic side of you, and will make you appreciate life from a whole new perspective. The appreciation for all things beautiful is embedded within the heart of its natives, and the country of France as a whole. Art is Paris' way of life, the way Kung Fu is to China.

Paris is widely known as the "city of light" because of its people's historic participation during the Age of Enlightenment – where Europeans began to become open-minded about everything, from art and science, to government and religion and basically all of the ideals that had occurred and continue to occur up to this day that advanced the human race forward. Its ability to adapt and thrive in changing times without abandoning entirely its historical roots is what makes Paris the best of both worlds.

Whether this is your first time to visit the art - driven city of Paris, or if this is one of the several trips you have made to this vibrant city, there's always something new and different to see. Whether it's the history, the sights, the fashion, the glamour, the food, or the people - a trip to Paris is always a worthy experience.

There is something for everyone - whether you're a history buff, an artist looking for an inspiration, an outdoors person looking for an adventure, someone who appreciates fashion, or one who just loves to eat French delicacies, Paris got it all for you!

In this book, you will learn the basic things you need to know about Paris – its location, its people, its language, culture and seasons. You will also be given information regarding your travel needs, and of course an overview of the top tourist attractions, hotels and food places as well as hidden facets of the city to meet your thirst for exploration.

So what are you waiting for? Get ready to pack your bags, your passport, and your pocket money! Let's set out for one of the most exciting places in the world that will never be out of anyone's bucket list! Bon Voyage!

Chapter One: Paris Overview

Before your plane lands on one of the most must-see cities in the world, it is essential to know intricate details of what you're about to deal with. Paris is quite a populated city in France, and if it is your first time to travel here, you might want to consider discovering facts about this awesome place, so that you know what to expect before you go about in your itinerary and to avoid getting into trouble. In this chapter, you will be provided with an overview of Paris – its city, language, culture, people, and history.

If you have enough knowledge about these things, you will not just enjoy and appreciate the city but also get to be prepared for a different kind of adventure – French style!

Paris in Focus

Paris is strategically located in the central northern region of France surrounded by two islands; the *Île Saint-Louis* and *Île de la Cité* . The city is generally flat and it is spread near one of the oldest river banks in the world called *La Manche* or the English Channel.

Paris is widely known as the "city of light," for two reasons; first, as mentioned earlier, Parisians who lived centuries ago were part of a European revolution called the Age of Enlightenment. This was the time when Europeans particularly intellectuals, and scholars as well as artists and philosophers began to advance a certain sense of ideals such as liberation, justice, religion, equality etc. that would later change and affect the way they live their lives and that of the world. The second main reason is simply because Paris was one of the first cities in the world to adapt gas street lighting that illuminated the different streets of the city in 1860.

In the past few years, Paris continues to become the central district for business and culture in France and in Europe. The city adapted to several economic changes and continues to become one of the key cities in the 21st century.

Paris is also regarded as one of the richest regions in all of Europe. It is still the center for trade, fashion, art, commerce and transportation that connects nearby cities of France.

The city also participated in major sporting events such as the Summer Olympics, FIFA World Cup, Rugby World Cup, and the famous *Tour de France*. The city is currently bidding to host the 2024 Summer Olympics.

A Brief History of Paris

Before Paris became the hub for artists and philosophers alike, and before it became the city that it is today it had gone through different phases and major changes; let's have a quick look at what went down in its history.

- **3rd century B.C.:** A tribe of Celtic fishermen, also known as the *Parisii* acquired an area near the fertile river bank called the Seine River.

- **52 B.C.:** Julius Ceasar acquired the city, and later became part of the Roman Empire, the territory was known as Gaul.

- **4th – 9th centuries:** The territory was seized by Clovis I, and renamed it Lutetia Paris.

- **1163:** Notre Dame Cathedral began construction during the era of gothic architecture. The cathedral was finished after almost two centuries.

- **12th and 13th century:** It started becoming as the medieval city; construction of famous sites such as the Sainte - Chapelle cathedral, Louvre, and Sorbonne begins.

- **Late 14th century:** the city's population was struck by a plague called the Black Death.

- **Late 15th century:** The age of rebirth or The Renaissance begins. The city was eventually became a center for art, architecture, technology and science.

- **Late 16th century:** there were a lot of religious conflicts particularly between the Catholics and Protestants that lead to the massacre of 3000 Protestants known as the St. Bartholomew's Day massacre.

- **1643:** 5 year old Louis XIV, becomes the King of France. During his rule, the Versailles was built and France became powerful and prosperous.

- **1774:** King Louis XVI come of age and officially ascended the throne. He then married Marie Antoinette, the daughter of an Austrian empress.

- **1792:** The fall of King Louis XVI's monarchy, and the first French republic was established. The King and his wife are guillotined after being accused of extensive decadence and indifference to its people.

- **1793-1799:** The "reign of terror" and chaos took place. A new calendar was formed and religion was banned.

- **1799:** General Napoleon Bonaparte aimed to stabilize the chaotic government, and later became emperor in 1804. He then colonized North Africa during his time, but power lead him astray. He was later defeated in 1815.

- **Mid-19th century:** Paris began renovating its city by re-constructing boulevards and replacing its sewage system under the Napoleon III.

- **1870:** After being defeated by the Prussians, the third republic was established and the democratic institutions began. The era of impressionism made its mark in the genre of arts. It was the beginning of Paris' golden age in artistic feats.

- **1920's and 1930's:** Art and literature in Paris took the world by storm and made its marks in history. Paris became home to famous artists' such as Pablo Picasso, Salvador Dali, and writers such as Ernest Hemingway, Gertrude Stein and James Joyce.

- **1940:** Nazi's invades Paris. France was occupied by Germany for over four years. A resistance movement was led by General Charles de Gaulle.

- **1944:** France was freed by the Allied Forces, World War II ends, and Hitler's Nazi Germany had fallen.

- **1945 – Present:** Paris became the center for arts, culture, science, fashion and business. A thriving metropolis in the heart of Europe.

Paris' Language, People and Culture

As soon as you step foot in this city, you will be immediately exposed to its vast artistic achievement, and grandiose architecture that stood the test of time. The world "culture" actually came from French term that originated from a Latin word *colere,* which means to grow and to cultivate. When you think of Paris, you think of art, and how it is applied in everyday life of the city. In this section, you will learn more about the kind of people you are going to mingle with, the culture that surrounds the city and the language that binds it all together. You will also learn why Paris is also called the "city of love."

Paris' rich cultures were mainly influenced by its first residents – the Parisii. They came from a Celtic background, mixed with a Gallo-Roman culture. However, the city's culture is also richly diverse and influenced by the Scandinavians, Romans and British. The city has now a population of over 2 million people, and in the European Union it is also the fifth largest municipality.

French is the official language used by Paris' residents, and it is also the second widely learned language in the world, although some will argue, that love is also its major language. Don't worry though; there are also lots of people who are speaking in English and can understand it.

Parisians, and French people in general takes great pride of their country and its government, they get offended if foreigners insult or has a negative comment about their nation. They are also in general very passionate and romantic people; their attitude towards sex outside of marriage is accepted. They are mostly sophisticated, and they are the kind of people who appreciates beauty and style in the most regal manner.

Paris became known as the "city of love and romance" for many reasons, one of which is because of its "romantic" ambience – the beautiful glow of the Eiffel Tower at night, the romantic walks in the historic Seine River, the love padlocks in Pont des Arts, the fine dining, the exquisite architecture, the luxury hotels, and the sweet French people. The language of love mainly encompasses the whole city, which is why lots of tourists especially couples are attracted to go to Paris and spend time with their loved ones.

Chapter Two: Travel Essentials

Now that you have learned several things about Paris and already have general knowledge of the city, the next thing for you to learn about and accomplish before actually going there is the travelling requirements or traveller's info.

The travel requirements and some basic reminders in planning your trip to this city are essential in order for you to have a wonderful experience and not get into trouble especially in immigration and customs.

In this chapter, you will learn what you need to do for you to be able to travel to Paris; things you need to bring and be aware of, the different transportations and ports of entry in and out of the city as well as essential information for first time travellers such as money, communication.

Visa and Passport Requirements

Just like other countries, a valid visa and updated passport is required for all visitors to the city. First and foremost, if you are a tourist, you need to have Schengen Visa (valid only for 90 days or 3 months). If you are planning to stay in France for more than 3 months, (either for work purposes or personal matters) then you need to apply for a long-stay visa provided that you have presented appropriate documents needed or reasons for your longer stay.

For the purposes of this book, the information that will be provided is only applicable for tourists in general, or people who'll only stay in Paris for a short time.

If you do not have a Schengen Visa yet, you need to apply for it by presenting your passport (it should be valid for at least three months after you have requested for a Schengen Visa; application forms (duly completed and properly signed) also need to be submitted together with other proof of documents required by the French embassy. There will be visa application fees that you need to pay depending on which country you are from. Please check it with the French embassy in your country.

Below is a list of additional proof of documents you may need to provide:

- Proof of the purpose of your stay in the Schengen area
- Proof of your means of support during your stay and accommodation
- Proof of travel and repatriation insurance
- Guarantees of repatriation to your country of residence (return ticket or adequate personal means to purchase one)
- For children under 18 years of age, specific proof; visa application forms must be signed by the parent or legal guardian
- Any documents helping to convince the consular authority of your intention to leave the Schengen area when your visa expires.

You can check the nearest French embassy in your area if you are unsure of your status. For further info regarding visa and passport requirements, please check the French consular website online.

As of now, there are only a few countries specified by the European regulation in France that are exempted from acquiring a Schengen Visa (provided that it is short – term stay only).

Here are the lists of nationals that are exempted from the visa requirement in France.

- Members or family members of the European Union (EU), the European Economic Area (EEA) of Switzerland
- Nationals of the following countries, whatever the reason for their stay:
    - Albania
    - Antigua and Barbuda
    - Argentina
    - Australia
    - Bahamas
    - Barbados
    - Bosnia and Herzegovina
    - Canada
    - Croatia,
    - Honduras
    - Japan
    - Mexico
    - Monaco,

  - New Zealand
  - Panama
  - South Korea
  - Uruguay
  - USA
  - Venezuela

  *For complete list of the countries or nationals that are exempted for a visa requirement under certain conditions, and for other exemptions (e.g. special cases, overseas department, immigrants etc.) please consult the consular website in your country.

- Holders of a valid residence permit for France

Visa Processing Time and Fees

The processing time will vary depending on your country or the local conditions of the issuing department. Please visit the consular website for further information regarding the processing duration.

You need to pay 60 Euros to apply for a Schengen (short – stay) Visa. Exemptions will apply for certain nationals, as well as members of the EU. If you are planning to apply for a long-stay visa, you will most likely pay 99 Euros. The application fees are non-refundable regardless if your visa application is approved or not.

*Application fees may change without prior notice.

Traveller's Info

In this section, you will be provided with essential traveler's information on what to do and what not to do in Paris. Be sure to keep all these essentials in mind while you are traveling.

Money Exchange, ATMs, and Credit Cards

The currency in France is called Euros. You may want to exchange your national money to any banks around Paris, or better yet to the exchange bureaus that can be found in almost all major attractions in the city, including the airport or other transportation hubs.

It is better to exchange for large sums of your money so you can get the best rates, usually the buying and selling rates is around 5%. If exchanging money at centers is too much hassle for you, you can also withdraw euros at an ATM machine (provided that your card is accepted).

ATMs are found almost everywhere and are available 24/7. You can also use international cards but it may not be acceptable in all of the ATM machines available.

Credit cards such as Visa and MasterCard are accepted in various hotels, restaurants, and shops. An American Express card may not be accepted everywhere. You can easily tell what credit cards are accepted in a particular place by checking out their displayed sticker.

Another important thing to remember is whenever you are paying at gas stations or within the metro using ticket machines make sure that your credit card has a chip, otherwise it may not be acceptable, if in case this happens, you can just pay in cash.

Electricity and Voltage

Paris' standard electrical voltage is 230 volts or 50 Hz AC. Majority of the plugs have two round pins. You may need a transformer or converter to aid your electrical equipment or appliances. You can buy adaptors at various convenience and electrical/gadget stores.

Public Holidays

Major shops and restaurants are usually open on weekdays until Saturday except during national holidays, such as New Year, Christmas Day, or during Holy Week.

Supermarkets are usually open until 8 PM, while major shopping avenues or boulevards stay open until midnight and even on Sundays especially if it is Christmas season, or the holidays.

Banks and public institutions are open daily until 6 PM. Museums are usually close on Mondays and Tuesdays, and on national holidays. Check their website before planning your trip

Health and Safety

You don't necessarily need vaccination certificates or other medical certificates upon entering in France, although it's better to check if your airline requires it. If you are a citizen of the EU, you must bring a certificate so you can reimburse about 70% of medical expenses.

If you happen to bring to your pets, you need to show its health or medical clearances to ensure that they have been vaccinated and free of rabies. Please also check the consular website regarding the breed or the type of animal you can bring to France.

- **Potable Water**

The municipal water in Paris is approved by the World Health Organization and therefore safe to drink. It is free for locals and tourists. Mineral waters, including imported brands, can be found in stores and supermarkets.

- **Hospitals**

Hospitals in Paris are readily available in case of any emergencies or accidents. The medical fee for attendance depends on the hospital and the procedure that will be done; patients will always be treated even if they cannot pay immediately. Most medical professionals in public and private sectors can speak in English.

- **Smoking restrictions**

Smokers are not welcome in Paris. The city is implementing a smoking ban both for indoors and outdoors in all public transportations and carriers, hotels, malls, restaurants, nightclubs, school premises, supermarket, parks, etc. since January 2008. If you got caught smoking in prohibited areas, you can get arrested and may need to pay a fee.

Safety Tips

- Do not leave your valuables unattended. Your money, passport or travel documents should be in a safe place, or you should carry it with you at all times.

- Be vigilant and watch out for your valuables especially in crowded places.

- Beware of thieves, the most common threat in France is pickpockets especially when riding the trains. Sometimes there are organized gang groups who are expert at pickpocketing. Some thieves snatches tourists' belongings directly and ran off, so you have to use your common sense and be wary at all times.

- Observe the rules and regulations of public places especially inside shopping malls and tourist spots

For your peace of mind, Paris is frequently patrolled by police officers and they are very helpful, nonetheless, you still need to stay alert and mindful at all times. You can also report to the French police if in case someone stole your belongings or for any serious issues.

Public Hygiene and Environmental Regulations

Here are some rules you need to follow while wandering around Paris.

- Do not eat or drink in public transportations.

- If you are caught littering, drunk driving or urinating in public venues, you will be fined by authorities or get arrested.

- Public washrooms are clean and sanitary. Follow the rules inside public toilets.

- Maintain cleanliness and clean as you go.

Customs

Upon arriving at the airport in Paris, you will need to be cleared by the department of customs. You must declare commodities and duty-free quotas. Here are some things to keep in mind:

- Importation and exportation of prohibited items such as dangerous drugs, firearms, weapons, plants, endangered species, and poultry must be accompanied by valid license, permit or certification issued in advance by relevant authorities unless exempted by law

- 'Mace Spray,' stun gun, tasers and other various personal protection devices, are also prohibited in Paris.

- Do not include sharp objects such as blades, cutters or knives in your carry-on luggage. Pack these items in your check – in luggage.

- Do not carry liquid substances such as gels, aerosols, perfumes, etc. that are bigger than 100ml. For these items, place it in a single transparent and re-sealable bag, only one bag per passenger is allowed.

Travel Insurance

It is highly recommended that you acquire travel insurance before traveling to Paris. Inquire with your travel insurance company about the emergency coverage, contact numbers, and persons as well as the insurance policy. If you already have one, always carry with you the insurance policy and the insurance company hotline number for identification purposes in cases of emergencies.

Communication Services

Another central necessity that you need to have access to is the transmission lines and services. Obviously, when you get to another country, the mobile services, as well as internet services, will be different. Here are some things you need to keep in mind for you to be able to communicate effectively while in Paris.

- **Mobile Phones**

There are four operators in France; the whole country is covered by GSM 900, 1800, GPRS, and HSPDA network. Some European phones will work, while tourist phones from other countries may not. Be sure to check for the compatibility. It's also highly recommended that you buy a cheap local sim card, so you can effectively communicate 24/7.

- **Wi-Fi/ Internet Services**

Who wouldn't want to tweet or share online about their trip to Paris? Aside from staying connected, I'm sure everyone especially tourists can't fight the urge to update the social media world and their online status regarding their whereabouts while spending time in the city of light!

No worries, Paris got you covered. There are over 400 hotspots around the city particularly in the primary public locations and tourist destinations such as department stores, theme parks, gardens, centers, restaurants and dining places, hotels, transportation terminals, government buildings and public venues that are free! All you have to do is to open your Wi-Fi and connect to 'Orange' network so that you can have free internet access.

Internet cafes are also available in various locations and you can find them easily.

Seasons in Paris

Now that you have accomplished everything you need and perhaps learned and prepared for the necessary traveling essentials, the only thing left to do it to set out an itinerary right? Well, not yet! There is still one major factor you need to consider – the climate. You don't want to go against Mother Nature so to speak, and you don't want to also ruin your trip by not being prepared regarding the weather.

In this section, you will learn what to expect in Paris' changing seasons so you can plan your trip accordingly.

Emergency Numbers

You may need to keep these emergency numbers on your phone just in case any issues arise while you are in Paris.

- **Emergency Medical Services: Service d'Aide Médicale Urgente (SAMU)** – dial 15 on the telephone
- **National Police** – dial 17 on the telephone
- **Fire Brigade** – dial 18 on the telephone
- **Poison Control Center** – dial 01 40 05 48 48
- **Lost and Found** – 08 21 00 25 25 – 36
- **Lost or stolen credit cards** – 0892 70 57 05
- **Removal of vehicle** – 08 91 01 22 22

Climate and Weather

The city of Paris has a temperate climate with mild winters and summers; the only possible event that can ruin your trip or postponed it is storms. Fortunately, storms are very predictable - thanks to weather channels and modern technologies.

Violent storms occasionally occur, usually during spring or summer. Of course, when there is one approaching the city, the government announces it on different media channels, which is why you should check the weather first before setting a date for your trip or booking a ticket.

There will be warning signals to alert the locals as well as international transportations that will be announced by the government.

Seasons

Below is a brief overview of the seasons you can get to experience while in Paris.

Spring (March 21 to June 21)

This is a great time to stroll in the park, visit the museums, and enjoy the scenery. The average temperature during spring is 10oC – 20oC.

Summer (June 21 to September 21)

This is the time to enjoy various fests in Paris; there are lots of free films and concerts around the capital. Also the best time to have picnic in the park, and relax in café terraces while admiring the ambience of the city. Average temperature during summer is 23oC – 24oC.

Autumn (September 21 to December 21)

The days are getting shorter, but the adventure is not. Tourists can enjoy major cultural shows, and fairs around the city. Average temperature during autumn is 15oC – 21oC.

Winter (December 21 to March 21)

Christmas is in full swing, major shopping centers, and restaurants are all geared up for the holidays. The streets of Paris are all covered with glamorous Christmas decorations. Best time for shopaholics out there and a great opportunity to indulge in Paris' best coffee shops. The average temperature during winter is 2oC – 7oC.

Chapter Three: Getting In and Around Paris

After learning the different requirements you need before traveling to this beautiful city, the next thing you should know is how to navigate around it. If you have enough knowledge regarding Paris' port of entry and transportation services, you will quickly get to your destination with ease. So don't waste your time, energy and money, they are precious, and they should only be consumed by the spirit of Paris. Learning how to navigate Paris is the key to finding great places, meeting amazing people and saving a lot of money and time for a unique and one-of-a-kind experience.

In this chapter, you will learn the major transportation systems and port of entries as well as communication services to help you reach and explore different tourist destinations as well as, far-flung places. So grab your map and look out on the horizon, Paris is waiting for you!

Traveling by Plane

Paris is one of the most connected cities in Europe and in the world. There are a lot of international airports in Paris such as the Charles de Gaulle Airport (main international airport), Orly Airport (second main international airport), and the Paris – Le Bourget Airport (original airport in the city). Your airline may also land at the Beauvais-Tillé Airport, it is the where budget airlines are located.

From there you can take the train or Metro, hail a cab, or ride a bus to get to your destination.

Traveling by Train

The Paris Metro train is the best mode of transportation to get around the city from the airport or if you are coming from your hotel. There are over 16 lines of trains scattered in Paris, with over 300 stations in total that are connected via different zones such as Zone 1, Zone 2, or Zone 3. The rail system operates from 5:30 AM to 12:40 AM

(Sunday to Thursday), the train operations on Fridays, Saturdays, and during holidays, run from 5:30 AM to 1:40 AM.

The train interval during rush hours is usually around 2 minutes. It may take around 8 to10 minutes during holidays, off-hours, and on Sundays.

The Réseau Express Régional (RER) or Regional Express Network is 5 special express railway systems that act as a subway train for people who want to go to the countryside or outside the capital. It is a suburban express railway that commuters take if you need to cross Paris quickly.

Fares for Metro: €1.90 (Single Journey); €16 (book of 10 tickets) valid for Zones 1 and 2.

Fares for RER: ticket prices are determined in every station, which usually ranges from €1.90 up to €12.05. The ticket is only valid for central Paris Zone 1. If you go beyond that you need to purchase another ticket called a *Billet Ile-de-France.*

Traveling by Buses

The buses in Paris are a great alternative if you want to go to specific places around town. There are 59 routes, and these buses also go to the suburbs. The bus system operates from 7 AM to 8:30 PM (Monday to Saturday), there are also night buses available called Noctilien that operates from 12:30 AM to 5:30 AM (Monday to Saturday). The schedule of buses during holidays may change or operation could be extended. Make sure to check their schedule as well.

The buses are consists of about 47 lines, and they can also bring you back to your hotel if in case you missed the last metro train. Standard fares apply. You will need a new ticket if you decide to change routes. It's also better to buy a travel pass or carnet (pack of ten tickets) if you plan to travel a lot via buses.

There are also lots of international buses that operate from and to Paris, especially if you are just coming from other parts of France or Europe.

Fares for Buses: around €1.90, same ticket price that you used in the Metro; valid for single journey only.

Traveling by Taxi

Just like buses, taxis or cabs are always available in the pick-up area of the airport. These taxis can also be hailed in the streets or contacted by phone for service. The universal number for calling a cab is +33 145 30 30 30. They are all metered, air-conditioned, fairly inexpensive and clean. The information regarding charges is often displayed inside the vehicle. Make sure that the taxi also has a license plate number to avoid getting scammed.

It is highly recommended that you take the metro train during the day because there's a huge chance that the roads are heavy. It is better though, to take a cab at night so you can have a quick and inexpensive ride or mode of transportation. Unfortunately, no supplements can be requested to aid persons with disability.

Here is the list of specially – equipped taxis according to the Department of Tourism in Paris:

- Must have an illuminated "Taxi Parisien" sign on the roof of the taxi
- Must have a display meter showing the cost of the journey
- Must have a display at the rear of the vehicle and visible from the exterior which enables the monitoring of the daily duration of use of the vehicle
- Must have a plate fixed to the front right-hand wing of the vehicle bearing the license number

Taxis that do not have the qualifications mentioned above are considered illegal. Do not ride in those cabs. Make sure to check it first.

Fares for Taxi: €5.50 - €7 (initial fare)

- Fares for succeeding or additional kilometers highly depend at the speed of the car, which will be shown by the meter.
- Tip is usually included but there could be additional charges for luggage usually around €1.

Traveling by Boat

For tourists who can splurge big time, you can also take a sightseeing tour around Paris particularly in the scenic Seine River via boat or cruise. The river boats will take you to an exclusive tour (translated both in French and English) so you can know more about the marvelous museums and monuments around the area.

You can also opt to have a romantic dinner or lunch while cruising the river by renting small boats or small yachts. Packages and prices vary and may change without prior notice.

Transport Travel Card

Transport Travel Cards functions as an unlimited pass allowing you to travel on the metro, bus, tramway, RER systems in Paris including its suburbs. This travel pass is best suited for tourists who wanted to explore the city further. Once you purchase a Transport Travel Card, it may be valid for 1, 2, 3 or for 5 consecutive days (depending on how long you think you need it). You can use it in Zones 1 to 5, including close suburbs. The pass can be use from 5:30 AM until 5:30 AM the following day. Prices for adults and children may vary.

Chapter Four: Hotels and Accommodations

After learning about the ports of entry in Paris and the different ways on how you can get around this beautiful city, the next thing you should know after arriving at the airport is where to stay. There are tons of options online and a lot of feedback from friends, and family who have stayed in the city - not to mention the thousands of social reviews and comments on different social networking sites.

The million dollar question is - where should you stay and how in the world are you going to choose the best accommodation in this vibrant city?

In this chapter you will be provided with the list of what we consider to be the top 10 best hotel districts in Paris. Some are very expensive, while others are a bit more cost-friendly. The variety of hotel accommodations you can probably expect may include any of the following:

- Hostels
- Bed & Breakfast
- Budget Hotels (2-3 star ratings)
- 4 Star Hotels
- 5 Star Hotels
- Apartments for short-term lease
- Rooms for rent
- Family Rooms for rent

If you want to know the best fit for you in every aspect – financial, proximity, ambiance and overall experience, check out the following recommended hotel areas or accommodation district below.

1. *Le Marais District*

Le Marais district is the best neighborhood in Paris. If it's your first time (or even if you've been to the city before), this is the best district in Paris that you should definitely stay in. The Marais district is also in central Paris which means you have an easy access to several tourist attractions, fine dinings and café shops. This is also a haven for shoppers; Le Marais has lots of world-renowned boutiques, and it has the greatest accommodations – not to mention the beautiful architecture around the area.

Le Marais is also one of the oldest districts in Paris; there is also the hub of LGBT and the Jewish community. If you go and stay here, you'll meet a lot of different people, diverse but united. It is also known as the "gay life" district in Paris. You can enjoy hanging out in trendy bars at night; visit the Louvre museum (former royal palace), have your pictures taken famous Louvre pyramid, shop for jewelries and clothing's in various malls, take a walk along Tuileries Gardens, or discover the collections at Center Pompidou.

The Le Marais is located in the 3rd and 4th district in the city. Here's a quick overview of the famous hotels as well as cheap accommodations around the Le Marais District in Paris:

- Le Pavillion de la Reine
- Hotel Jules & Jim
- Hotel du Petit Moulin
- Les Tournelles Paris
- Appartement Gravilliers 12
- Apartment Temple
- Le Marais Private Homes
- Place des Vosges
- Studio Temple
- Le Comte Studio

2. *St. Germain - des - Pres District*

St. Germain des Pres is another great district that you should opt to stay in, while you and your loved ones are in Paris. There are lots of tourists in this area, and what's great about it is that you can indulge yourself from its famous and long-time cafés, little French shops, and maybe have a chat with the people around; the streets are packed with interesting stories, so if I were you I'd really talk to them and get to know them. Some of the attractions that are near the district are the Jardin du Luxembourg, Notre Dame, and the

Musée d'Orsay. Another great thing about this district is that it is home to the oldest and historic publishers and bookstores in France. For all you bookworms and historians out there, it is highly recommended that you checked-in in this district so you can really satisfy your intellectual cravings!

There are also lots of artistic events such as art fests, exhibits, concerts, jazz clubs etc. that is constantly happening around the area. This district is the hub of writers and artists in Paris. You might get to meet the next Picasso or Hemingway here. It is located in the 6th district in Paris.

Here's a quick overview of the famous hotels as well as cheap accommodations around the St. Germain des Pres district of Paris:

- Hotel Madison by MH
- Bel-Ami Hotel
- Artus Hotel by MH
- Hotel de l'Academie
- Hotel Left Bank Saint Germain
- Hotel De Buci by MH
- Hotel de Saint-Germain
- Au Manoir Saint Germain
- Crystal Hotel Paris
- Grand Hotel de L'Univers Saint-Germain

3. *Montmartre District*

Montmartre district can be a bit tricky especially for first time tourists. It's a great district to stay in, but you have to make sure that you are in the "good side" of the neighborhood. Most of it is an urban neighborhood, much like a village, but the "dark side" of it may not impress you, especially the areas around Pigalle. The side street in Rue Lepic is amazing, but the Boulevard Clichy is full of sex shops. This kind of neighborhood may not be suitable for families especially with small children.

It is highly recommended that research first the area or hotel that you're going to stay in in Montmartre. There are lots of great accommodations at cheaper prices around the area as well as various boutiques, and restaurants. It is located in the 18th district of Paris

Here's a quick overview of the famous hotels around the Montmartre district of Paris:

- Mercure Paris Montmartre Sacre Coeur
- Ibis Paris Montmartre
- Hotel Le Chat Noir
- Le Grand Hotel De Clermont
- Hotel des Arts - Montmartre Paris
- Hotel Montmartre Sacre-Coeur
- Citadines Montmartre Paris
- The Modern Hotel
- Hipotel Paris Gare du Nord Merryl
- Hipotel Paris Sacre Coeur Olympiades

4. 9th District

If you would like a little peace and quiet, the 9th arrondissement is highly recommended for you. There are not a lot of tourists staying around the area, so this is easily the place where you can meet authentic Parisians! It may not look like a cool neighborhood like the other districts but it's a great place to stay in as well while you are in Paris.

Its location is quite strategic, and could be a great base for you to start exploring the off beaten part of the city. It is also a residential zone, and it is near Montmartre district as well. There are also plenty of bars, restaurants, cafes, and some shopping establishments that mostly cater to Parisians and not to tourists. If you choose to stay in this place though, there aren't a lot of attractions near the area, but it is a great place if you truly want to meet the people of France.

Here's a quick overview of the famous hotels around the 9th district of Paris:

- Hotel de Nell
- Residence Nell
- Residence Nell
- Hotel France Albion
- 9hotel Opera
- Hotel Chateaudun Opera
- Hotel Alize Montmartre
- Libertel Montmartre Opera
- Hotel Scribe Paris Opera by Sofitel
- Hotel Antin Trinite
- Le Grand Hotel de Normandie

5. *Ile Saint - Louis District*

Ile Saint – Louis district is located at the center of Paris. This neighborhood is a cozy place to stay in, and what's great about it is that it is near great establishments and famous attractions. It almost feels like a small town even if there are lots of tourists on the other side. It is near the Notre Dame, and also has lots of authentic French restaurants, café shops, various boutiques, and lots of Parisians and tourists in between. If you wanted to be at the heart of Paris but still sort of like wanted to have a bit of privacy and breather from all the tourists out there Ile Saint

– Louis district is the best choice for you. There are also lots of great accommodations and hotel you can choose from. It is located in the 4th district of Paris.

Here's a quick overview of the famous hotels around the Ile Saint – Louis district of Paris:

- Hotel Saint-Louis en l'Isle
- Hotel des Deux Iles
- Hotel du Jeu De Paume
- Studio on the Ile Saint Louis
- HA'tel des Deux Iles
- Apartment Saint-Louis
- Apartment Quai de Bourbon
- Notre Dame - Ile Saint-Louis Private Homes
- Ile St Louis 4 personnes

6. Belleville District

If you wanted to find the hipsters of Paris, or you are looking for the Williamsburg version of Paris, then look no further! Go to Belleville and choose a hotel in the area.

The district is a hub for artists and entrepreneurs as well, there are lots of interesting and one – of – a – kind shops wherein you can find the cheapest items, and there are plenty of ethnic communities surrounding the area. It is a diverse place, and home to the working class residents of Paris. Since this place is full of people from different cultural and ethnic background, the restaurants and establishments nearby are also as diverse as the people it is surrounded with. You can definitely enjoy your stay at this fine place, it is easily accessible, and has lots of accommodations that can suit your budget.

Hotels and accommodations in Belleville district is much more affordable for tourists, here's a quick overview of hotels you could stay in around the area:

- Campanile Paris 19 - La Villette
- Libertel Canal Saint-Martin
- Holiday Inn Express Paris Canal De La Villette
- Forest Hill Paris La Villette
- St Christopher's Inn Paris - Canal
- Ibis Paris La Villette Cite Des Sciences
- Hotel ibis budget Paris La Villette
- B&B Hotel Porte des Lilas
- B&B Hotel Porte des Lilas
- Aparthotel Adagio Paris Buttes Chaumont

7. *Opera District*

If you have the money to splurge, and will settle for nothing but the best accommodation in this beautiful city, then the Opera district is one of the best choice for you!

The Opera district is a classy neighborhood, and it is located in the business district of Paris. This is considered as the most chic places in Paris, a hub for fashion designers, and a source of inspiration for aspiring artists, architects, and models of the 21st century.

There are lots of grandiose hotel around the area, and if you are part of the "rich and famous society," you'll surely enjoy the place. There is also ballet and opera nights in the theaters nearby like the Opera Garnier. If you are a shopaholic, this is where you can find famous and authentic brands of French clothing and Parisian fashion as well as Japanese brands. Boutiques such as Chanel, Cartier, Boucheron, Laduree, Fauchon etc. can be found in this district. The place is also near several tourist spots such as the Louvre, Plaza de al Madelaine, Place Vendome, Madelaine Church, and Palais Royal.

Locals and tourists alike said that once you stay here you'll definitely feel the Napoleonic power, and see the magnificent architectural feat of Haussmann Paris. It is located in the 8th arrondissement of Paris.

There are lots of 5 star hotels in Opera district as well as inexpensive accommodations for tourists (although there's not too many), here's a quick overview of hotels you could stay in around the area:

- Opera Opal
- Holiday Inn Paris Gare de L'Est
- Opera Liege
- Maison Albar Hotel Paris
- Opera Fauborg
- Aulivia Opera
- Ouest Hotel

8. Champs Elysees

If you think that Opera district is not enough, and you really saved up for this Paris trip, or you're just plain rich, then you may prefer to stay at one of the most beautiful avenue in the world! The Champ Elysees is the most iconic district in Paris, and in all of Europe. It is also the most luxurious and exquisite neighborhood that you can find, and it will take you straight in the heart of Paris. It is also the major axis of the city, which connects different districts, and is near lots of famous tourist attractions including the Eiffel Tower, Jeu de Paume, and the Arc de Triomphe. As you can imagine, there's a bounty of fine restaurants, the most luxurious boutiques and fashion stores, historical museums and iconic establishments. The district pretty much captures the spirit of Paris, and its elegance. You are really fortunate if you can book a hotel here. Lots of tourists from around the world love to stay in this district for their Paris trip. This is also the hub for fashion designers, entrepreneurs and artists. Don't forget to stroll along the Promenade Plantee, and shop for fresh food at the Aligre market.

Here's a quick overview of the famous hotels Champ Elysees district of Paris:

- Elysee Secret
- Elysees Mac Mahon Hotel
- The Beauchamps Hotel

9. *Gare de Lyon District*

The Gare de Lyon district is one of the most relaxing and quiet places in Paris. If you wanted to escape the hustle and bustle of the city, then it's probably best for you to stay here for your trips duration.

The Gare de Lyon is near the Marais and Bastille district, there are lots of bars, nightclubs, shopping stores, restaurants surrounding the area. It is also pretty accessible, and major tourist attractions are just a couple of minutes away because of its strategic location and transportation connections via the RER and its subway.

If you are into opera or theatrical performances, you can check out Opera Bastille, or maybe have a shopping spree at the Faubourg Saint Antoine Street, take a walk in the Jardin des Plantes or visits of the National Museum of Natural History.

It is also a great idea to take your family out at the Vincennes Castle or walk them through the Bois de Vincennes. It is located in district 11 and 12 in Paris.

Here's a quick overview of the famous hotels near the Gare de Lyon district of Paris:

- 61 Paris Nation Hotel
- Saint Louis

10. Wagram Monceau

The last but definitely not the least is Wagram Monceau. It's also an area near the Champ Elysees, and it is another great and elegant district that you can stay in while you are wandering around the beautiful sights of Paris. Its location is close to various tourist destinations, very accessible, and also connects you to other major districts in Paris such as the Opera district. Probably the only difference between the Wagram Monceau district and Champ Elysees is that it is more peaceful, and more of a residential area that offers almost the same Parisian architecture experience. While you are staying here it is highly recommended by both locals and tourists alike that you grab a breakfast or lunch at the famous Jacquemart-Andre museum café, shop at the Rue Poncelet Market, and stroll at the Batignolles district. It is located in the 17th arrondissement of Paris, and the atmosphere in this area is truly unforgettable.

Here's a quick overview of the famous hotels near the Wagram Monceau district of Paris:

- Hotel de Neuville
- Opera Batignolles
- Maison Albar Hotel

Chapter Five: Fine Dining

Once you have decided what district you're going to stay in for your trip, the next thing you should know is the places where you could eat that are near shopping malls, or tourist attractions at the same time.

The second greatest thing that you can do while you are in Paris is to eat! Eat your heart out to the most delicious and savory European cuisine in the world. Paris is home to world – renowned restaurants, bars, café, and international cuisines. Brace yourself for a day of Parisian gastronomy!

In this chapter, we've put together the list of the top 10 dining districts in and around Paris that you should not dare miss! Bon Appetit!

1. 11th Arrondissement

The 11th arrondissement in Paris is without a doubt the best district you can eat your heart out! Hands down! If you are in a hurry or you're only in Paris for a limited time, or you only have a budget for a couple of restaurants, then this is the place you shouldn't dare miss!

The 11th district is now Paris' new hub for foodies. There are lots of newly open bars and bistro, and several eclectic and authentic French restaurants. This district is a Parisian's choice. It's also a cool neighborhood to stay in.

You can get gluten-free cookies, tacos partnered with a special coffee, cakes and cocktail on the rooftop while overseeing the whole district. This is also a great place to dine during the night, there is lots of fine wine, and beer lovers come to this place as well. It's a district where everyone can enjoy, where everyone can relate to, and savor the taste of Paris and of France.

Here's a quick overview of the restaurants and bars you need to check out while in the 11th district:

- Le Chateaubriand
- Au Passage
- Bones
- La Cave de Septime
- Le Servan
- Yard
- Cafe Chilango
- Thank You My Deer
- Chambelland
- Le Perchoir
- La Fine Mousse
- La Buvette

2. 10th Arrondissement

The 10th arrondissement is the second best place you can go to if you wanted to taste the best of Paris. Best part is, it is just near the 11th district, so if you are not yet satisfied, then you can head over here, and enjoy lots of fine restaurants that are also suited for the whole family.

This district is also the hub for vegetarians out there! You can take a breakfast here French style, drink awesome French liquors, and just check out the different famous French restaurants and bars around the area.

Here's a quick overview of the restaurants and bars you need to check out while in the 10th district:

- Chez Michel
- Chez Casimir
- La Pointe du Grouin
- Holybelly
- Sol Semilla
- Abri
- Hai Kai
- CopperBay
- Le Syndicat
- Bar Le COQ

3. *8th Arrondissement*

The 8th arrondissement is home to high – end, and tripled star restaurants in the city. The best part about this district is that, the food is of great quality at a much affordable price. The neighborhood is also a great place to stay in. The district is mostly surrounded with world –

renowned French institutions or restaurants that goes way back, by way back, I mean it has been there since the 1930's, passed on from one French family generation to another! If you'd like to experience Paris before the era of modern food, this is the place you should go to. It is also a favorite food hub of Parisians.

Here's a quick overview of the restaurants and bars you need to check out while in the 8th district:

- Alain Ducasse au Plaza Athénée
- Epicure
- Pierre Gagnaire
- Lasserre
- Apicius
- Le Cinq
- Le Taillevent
- Le Forum

4. 9th Arrondissement

If you love drinking cocktails, and are into mixology, then look further than the 9th arrondissement! This is where the art meets the spirit of drinking!

You can surely enjoy hanging out here with your buddies, especially at night while overlooking the beautiful city and gazing at the marvelous architecture that surrounds the area.

Lots of notable restaurants and bars are located here, and the best part is that you don't need reservation! You can enjoy tasting the classic European drinks, and also the 21st century mixology inspired from the Western culture. Bars are bountiful in this area of the city, just be sure not to get so drunk so you won't be caught by the French police!

Here's a quick overview of the restaurants and bars you need to check out while in the 9th district:

- Le Richer
- Caillebotte
- Glass
- Dirty Dick
- Artisan
- Baton Rouge
- Lulu White

5. 2nd Arrondissement

The 2nd arrondissement is another go-to place for Parisians and tourists alike, simply because there are lots of authentic French restaurants here that stood the test of time! The Rue de Nil is where you can find several classic restaurants in Paris. It's also a great district to stay in; there are lots of awesome apartments, and hotel around the area. Lots of famous European delicacies can also be found here, as well as fresh salads, and classic burgers. Since this place is packed with tourists almost every day especially at night, you may want to have a reservation first so you can have a great time dining here with your loved ones.

Here's a quick overview of the restaurants and bars you need to check out while in the 2nd district:

- Frenchie
- Frenchie to Go (around Rue de Nil)
- Saturne
- Ducasse's Aux Lyonnais
- Chez Georges
- Big Fernand
- Blend
- Racines

6. 6th Arrondissement

The 6th arrondissement is located in the awesome neighborhood of Saint Germain. It is also known as the top food destination for first time tourists in the city. Meat lovers, modern diners, cafes, bars, and sweet French delicacies can be found here.

You will never run of the places to eat and choose from in this district, it has something for everyone. Lots of famous French restaurants are also located in the area, this is the epicenter of tourists that are hungry for French cuisine!

There are also clubs around the area, where you and your friends can hang out during the night.

Here's a quick overview of the restaurants and bars you need to check out while in the 6th district:

- Le Relais de l'Entrecôte
- Le Comptoir du Relais
- Le Timbre
- Cafe Trama
- Fish La Boissonnerie
- Prescription Cocktail Club
- Laduree
- Henri Leroux
- Pierre Marcolini
- Patrick Roger.

7. 3rd Arrondissement

If you wanted to taste the world's best international cuisines in the heart of Paris, then the 3rd arrondissement is the place to go! This is probably the most diverse group of restaurants in the city. It is also where the oldest market in France is located; you can shop for fresh foods, and then take a break at the thriving stalls around the area.

This is the place where you can eat France's world – renowned buckwheat crepes, and French pastries. As mentioned earlier, the district is also full of different restaurants that have the most diverse specialties around the world. Here you can eat authentic Mexican tacos and guacamole, tastes the awesome American BBQ, and chill with cool European cocktails.

Here's a quick overview of the restaurants and bars you need to check out while in the 3rd district:

- Marché des Enfants Rouge
- Breizh Cafe
- Candelaria
- The Beast
- Le Mary Celeste
- Little Red Door

8. 1st Arrondissement

The 1st arrondissement is a great place to dine after you stroll around the marvelous Palais Royal, and Louvre. The Rue Sainte – Anne is where Parisians go if they wanted to taste an Asian cuisine, there's a famous Japanese restaurant around the area that foodies in Paris goes to. There are also lots of iconic cocktail and wine bars around the area; this is also a hub of chicken lovers. It is also the place where you can find the most Michelin – star restaurants. Lots of tourists come and go here because it is very accessible, and also located in the heart of Paris.

Here's a quick overview of the restaurants and bars you need to check out while in the 1st district:

- Willi's
- Verjus
- Le Meurice
- Yam'Tcha
- La Dame de PIC

9. 18th Arrondissement

The 18th arrondissement is an interesting place to dine in, because it is located in Montmartre, which is both a dichotomy of a tourist hub, and Paris' off - beaten – path. This is where you can find sold Parisian meals. It is also home to British cuisines, as well as cuisines from South America such as Venezuela.

You can also find lots of craft beer spots around the area, which is why it's also a great hub for friends during the night. Before you explore Paris' hidden facets, why not try to dine in this district first? Consider it an appetizer for what Paris' can offer!

Here's a quick overview of the restaurants and bars you need to check out while in the 18th district:

- Le Grand 8
- Miroir,
- Jeanne B
- Le Bal Cafe
- Bululu Arepera
- Le Supercoin
- À La Bière Comme à la Bière,
- La Brasserie de la Goutte d'Or

10. 4th Arrondissement

The last but definitely not the least is the 4th arrondissement. It is known for one of the most famous and traditional foods in France called the falafel. This is the place where you can find the most legit European cuisines smack right in the center of Paris; there are lots of Italian and Portuguese restaurants. There are also lots of new restaurants that offers an authentic Arabic, and Middle – Eastern cuisine. You can eat unlimited pastas, gelato, cocktails, falafel, beers, crepes and a whole lot more! If you're in this district, you can't get more European than this.

Here's a quick overview of the restaurants and bars you need to check out while in the 4th district:

- L'As Du Fallafel
- Miznon
- Pozzetto
- Comme à Lisbonne
- Sherry Butt
- Demory's

Chapter Six: Shopping in Paris

After eating your heart out and tasting the best French cuisine that Paris could offer, we now go to the next best thing that truly defines this city – fashion!

It is an injustice if you go to Paris, and not shop for clothes, even if it's just "window shopping." This is the fashion capital of France, of Europe, and of the world! (at least in most people's opinion!). When you speak about fashion, the city of Paris will never go out of style.
This is the city where shoppers die and go to shopping paradise! Literally shop 'til you drop.

In this chapter, we'll give you top ten of the best shopping districts that you should definitely check out while you are in Paris. Once you shop in Paris, you'll never look at fashion the same way again. Brace yourself for a fun – filled day, glamour is the name of the game!

1. Avenue des Champs Elysees

Let's start off in the heart of Paris – the famous Champs Elysees Avenue. In this part of town, fashion and shopping are the only thing that you should be doing!

The Champ Elysees Avenue is home to the most famous, respected and world – renowned fashion boutiques and shopping centers. If you wanted to find a ready – to wear outfit that is both luxurious and prestigious, then look no further, Champ Elysees got it all for you! This is the place where you can find the best in haute couture. You can also find lots of glamorous accessories for men and women, as well as high – end clothing, women's lingerie and footwear. This is the hub for fashion designers, fashion entrepreneurs, models, and shopaholics! The spring collection in this town is one of the most anticipated events in fashion.

You can also find lots of restaurants, coffee bars, cinemas and department stores around where you can chill and relax after exhausting yourself from all these glamour.

The avenue is near George V, avenue Montaigne, and another famous shopping establishment called the Porte Maillot.

Here's a quick overview of the famous boutiques and shopping stores you need to check out while you are in Avenue des Champs Elysees:

- Louis Vuitton
- Dior
- Hugo Boss
- Chanel
- Kenzo
- Ralph Lauren

- Maison Saint Laurent Paris
- Marks & Spencer
- Tiffany & Co.
- Banana Republic
- Levi's
- Manoush
- La Marque de Maquillage
- MAC
- Guerlain
- Hermès
- Swarovski
- IKKS
- Éric Bompard
- Emilio Pucci
- Dior Homme
- Celine
- Gucci
- Jil Sander
- Emanuel Ungaro
- Valentino
- Malo
- Marni
- Nina Ricci
- Chloé
- Paul & Joe
- Blumarine
- Roberto Cavalli
- Atelier Renault
- H&M
- Tommy Hilfiger
- Abercrombie & Fitch
- Le Royal Éclaireur
- Giorgio Armani
- Dolce & Gabbana
- Gianni Versace

2. *Rue de Rennes*

Next stop is Rue de Rennes, which is located also in central Paris alongside the famous neighborhood of Saint – Germain des Pres, and Sevres - Babylone. This is another great place to shop especially if you wanted to find the best bags and shoes around town. Just like the Champ Elysees avenue, there are also lots of famous brands surrounding this road, from chic fashion, to corporate attires as well as women's accessories, and men's apparel. The large window displays in this road will surely attract even the non-shoppers. You can also find several Parisian pastry shops and French delicacies around the area such as Meert, and the famous La Tarte Tropézienne.

It's a long street, so be sure to use comfortable shoes if you are planning to check out this road. The best part is it is near the beautiful garden of Jardin du Luxembourg. After shopping you can drop by this awesome place so you can take a break from the hustle and bustle of the city, and take a breather in this lush garden.

Here's a quick overview of the famous boutiques and shopping stores you need to check out while you are in Rue de Rennes (Saint – Germain des Pres):

- Etam
- H&M
- Gap
- Kookaï
- Giorgio Armani
- Sonia Rykiel
- Christian Dior
- Ralph Lauren
- A.P.C.
- Carven
- Vicomte A
- Jérôme Dreyfuss
- Karl Lagerfeld
- Caroll
- Havaianas
- Ice Watch
- Edward Edward

3. *Haussmann – Opera*

Famous shops and department stores in Haussmann are strategically located between the Havre Caumartin and Chaussee d'Antin metro stations in the 9th district. You can't miss it because it's behind another famous establishment called the Paris Opera Garnier.

The Haussmann – Opera district is home to Paris' oldest and popular shopping center called the Galeries LaFayette. The district is popular for its urban and casual fashion wear. It is also the genuine commercial heart of the city.

The Galeries LaFayette offers a combination of high – end fashion accessories and apparels, as well as the various latest fashion trends for both men and women. You can also buy cosmetics, and hair accessories as well as branded watches or timepiece.

For all the millennial out there, you can also shop for the trendiest teenage fashion for a much cheaper price. Several Japanese fashion brands that specialize in chic outfit, clothes in cashmere and jumpers are also inside the department store.

You can also shop for non – fashion items such as furniture, products, and household items in this district. It is highly recommended that you do your shopping here at night because the building is lighted up in all its glory. This street is buzzing specially during a fashion sale, or whenever a new shopping centers open up (which is pretty much all the time).

Here's a quick overview of the famous brands and shopping stores you need to check out while you are in Haussmann – Opera:

- Galeries Lafayette
- Lafayette Maison
- Printemps
- Alexander McQueen
- Prada
- Louis Vuitton
- Eric Bompard
- Petit Bateau
- Lush
- L'Occitane
- Muji
- Red Valentino
- Bell & Ross
- Jaeger-LeCoultre
- Longines

- Uniqlo
- Maje

4. Rue de Rivoli - Le Marais

If originality is what you're seeking for or if you happen to be one of the last hipsters of this modern era then the district of Le Marais particularly in Rue de Rivoli is the go-to place for you! This is one of the longest streets in Paris, so better gear up for a very long walk. Don't worry though; you won't feel tired strolling along this road because you'd be entertained with all the famous and historical boutiques, and shopping centers that stood there since the Middle

Ages! Some of Paris' authentic clothing lines, brand of perfumes and designer shoes started here. For all the collectors out there, you can also find old antique shops that sell various and one – of – a – kind items.

The road is also famous for selling various luxury cosmetic items, hair accessories, souvenirs, and decorative objects. There are also lots of stores for kids' apparel. There are tons of coffee shops and restaurants around the area that you can go to after a day full of fun.

The Rue de Rivoli is a highly regarded street for Parisians and tourists alike, its avant – garde reputation is what made Le Marais a significant part of Paris.

Here's a quick overview of the famous brands and shopping stores you need to check out while you are in Rue de Rivoli (Le Marais):

- COS
- Eleven Paris
- Erotokritos
- Matières à réflexion
- The Kooples Sport
- Suite.341
- Maje
- Sandro
- Claudie Pierlot
- MAC
- Acqua di Parma
- Diptyque
- Guerlain
- Jo Malone
- The Haut Marais
- Sandro
- Stella Cadente
- Merci
- Bonton
- Forever 21

5. Rue des Martyrs

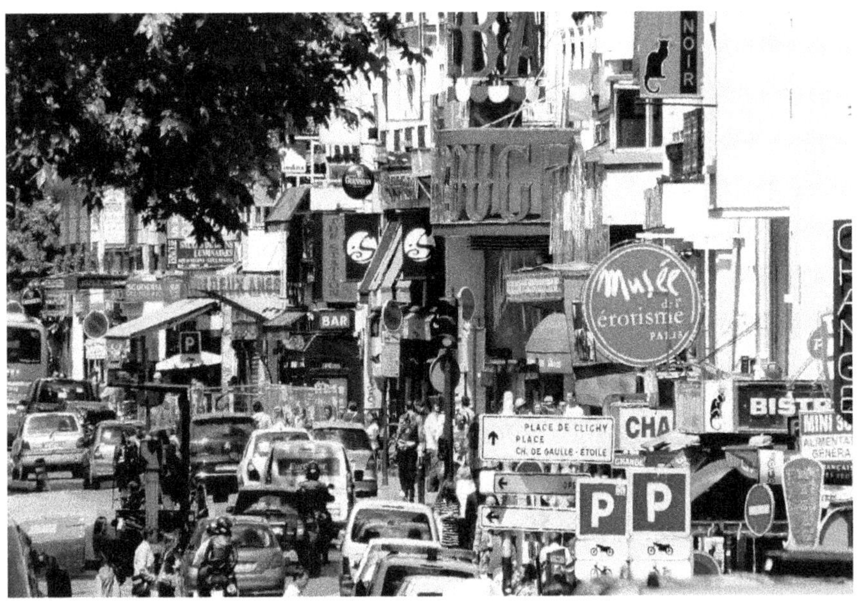

The Rue des Martyrs is not like any shopping areas in Paris. There's a sense of community around this area, it's cozy, it doesn't appear glamorous on the outside, but you can find lots of vintage boutiques and very tiny shopping stores in this area. This part of town is also known for its "bobo spirit," bobo means bourgeois bohemian. The bobo atmosphere is a very trendy fashion style in this area, so if you are into something that speaks diversity in the 'techy' 21st century this is the place suited for you.

There are tons of vintage shops that offer clothing lines, jewelries, shoes, and fashion products for men, women and kids. You can also find cheap cosmetics around the area, and if ever you wanted to have a relaxing time amidst all the chic lifestyle of Paris, you can drop by at Rue des Martyrs and beautify yourself because there are also tons of open nail bars, and beauty room where you can get your nail polish with your girlfriends.

The Rue des Martyrs is located in So-Pi or south of Pigalle, which also one of Paris' up and coming fashion district. You can also stop by for a quick snack and order up the famous French baguette at the popular Delmon Tel, or grab a healthy salad and sandwich at the Causses grocer.

Here's a quick overview of the famous brands and vintage stores you need to check out while you are in Rue des Martyrs (Pigalle):

- Zac & Sam
- Chezelle
- Chiffon & Basile
- Karine Arabian
- L'Œuf
- Bourjois

6. Rue Saint-Honoré

Classy and vintage is what Rue Saint – Honore is all about. This is the road for all you young – at – hearts out there, and youngsters too!

You can find tons of trendy fashion outfits, and apparels suited for corporate events, elegant parties, and formal gatherings. This is the place where you can also find the most extraordinary and fragrant perfumes customized just for you. This is also the hub for all the gentlemen out there, because there are tons of boutiques that offer men's fashion such as matching suits, neckties, and shoes. Similarly this also the place for all the lovely ladies as this road offers boutiques that sell those famous little black dresses.

This is also home to Paris' top designers, fashion icons that offer nothing but the most cutting – edge clothing lines and luxury items. Prepare to splurge all your money if you choose to shop for clothes in this road. It is sort of mainly exclusive for the rich and famous, although there are also quality department stores around the area that are affordable. You can also drop by at the famous emporium called the Colette, where you can find several clothing lines, bookshops, electronic stores and food stalls.

This road is situated between the Louvre and Opera, and near the Palais Royal. After shopping to your heart's content, you can chill and go to the popular Palais Royal, so you can imbibe the classy, elegant and royal spirit of Paris.

Here's a quick overview of the famous brands and classic stores you need to check out while you are in
Rue Saint - Honore:

- Didier Ludot
- Rick Owens and Stella McCartney
- Montpensier Galleries
- Valois Galleries
- Jérôme L'Huillier.
- Jovoy
- Pierre Hardy
- Jimmy Choo
- Christian Louboutin
- Maje
- Kitsuné
- H&M
- & Other Stories (sister company of H&M)

7. Montmartre District

Montmartre is sort of like an off – the beaten – path fashion district in Paris, simply but lots of tourists still come here to check out its jewelry and accessory shops. You can also find a good cultural fashion mix in this area, from Europe to Latin America. This place is suited for people looking for costumes, clothes for festive events, and accessories for artistic endeavors.

The vibrant splash of colors surrounds the area perfect for tourists who wanted to take a break from the high – end luxury shopping in central Paris.

You can also find souvenir shops, gift shops, and cool items that you can bring home. There are also lots of art galleries around, that's why this district is also the hub for artists, and craftsmen. This place also offers various pastry shops that you can go to such as one of the famous chocolate store called Maison Georges Larnicol, their specialty is a chocolate Eiffel Tower!

Here's a quick overview of the famous accessory brands and cool stores you need to check out while you are in Montmartre District:

- La Petite Maroquinerie
- Tienda Esquipulas
- Ba&sh
- Kookaï
- Sandro
- Karl Marc John
- Spree

8. Rue de Passy

Rue de Passy is one of the oldest department stores in Paris. It is located in the 16th arrondissement and also known for being one of the busiest shopping streets in the city. The fashion style here is classy but casual, perfect for teens and youngsters. The whole road is a one – way, narrow and long, you will definitely exhaust yourself so don't forget to prep up for it. This is also a hub for children's wear; there are lots of boutiques that offer the trendiest fashion style for kids. The road also has various garment stores from clothes, dress, pants, coats, shoes, accessories, and even furniture, souvenirs, gift shops, home decorations, and toys.

Aside from several French restaurants and dining places, there are also lots of food stalls around the malls, and you can also get Chinese food, and American fast foods in this area if in case you had enough of European cuisine (why would you?)

For you to get to this area, you can ride the Paris Metro and get off the Passy La Muette station.

Here's a quick overview of the famous apparel brands and department stores you need to check out while you are in Rue de Passy:

- Passy Plaza
- El Ganso
- Isabelle Marant (near Victor Hugo Avenue)
- Gap
- H&M
- Okaïdi
- Lacoste Woman
- Ekyog
- Eleven Paris
- Maje
- Repetto

9. Avenue des Ternes

The Avenue des Ternes is located in the energetic and vibrant 17th arrondissement; the best part about this district is that it is not as crowded like the other shopping districts in Paris. There aren't a lot of tourists, mostly Parisians shop here that is why it is also known as the commercial heart in the west of Paris. You can have the luxury of space, and time. Shop like a real Parisian and enjoy the walks like a native.

There are lots of popular brands both locally and internationally that offers almost everything you need such as high – end to low – end clothes, shoes, accessories, colorful shirts, shades, vintage dresses, gifts shops and even bookstores. There are also newly open malls targeted for future moms where you can also buy gifts for infants, and baby apparels. There are about 80 shops in one mall alone that are open from Monday until Sunday! You'll never run out of a shopping place if you are staying near the area.

Here's a quick overview of the famous apparel brands and department stores you need to check out while you are in Avenue des Ternes (17th District):

- Porte Maillot
- Parc Monceau
- Paul & Joe Sister
- Loft Design By
- Sandro
- Maje
- Les Petites
- Eric Bompard
- Nodus
- Bastien de Almeida
- Firmaman
- French Touche

10. Quartier Beaubourg et Les Halles

The incredible architectural structure of the Pompidou Center will surely seduce you to shop here. The place is also known as Quartier Beaubourg et Les Halles, and although there are many separate boutiques and clothing stores around the area, this is the flagship mall and go-to place of shoppers in the 4st arrondissement. Not only big brands and luxury stores are located here, there are also lots of clothing shops that offers the most diversified and eclectic outfits for an affordable price.

Another interesting fact about this district is that there is an underground shopping center that was once a hub for drug dealers, but don't worry, it's a safe place now, and lots of tourists also do their shopping there because aside from different chain stores, the products are very inexpensive and an open space as well.

You can also find various office supplies, household items, textile, and other chic items aside from clothes and apparel in Beauborg. So if you are into an interesting and weird shopping experience, you might want to check out not just the famous Pompidou Center but also the underground stores located at the Halles Forum.

Here's a quick overview of the famous apparel brands and chain stores you need to check out while you are in Quartier Beaubourg et Les Halles (1st arrondissement):

- Aigle
- Sixth June Paris
- Aldo
- Bourjois
- Calzedonia
- Officina
- Traffic soft furniture
- Claire's
- Du Pareil Au Meme
- Gap
- Geox
- Herschel
- H&M
- Kiki Make Up Milano
- Lacoste
- Levis
- L'oreille Cassee
- Maisons du Monde

- Pandora
- Passionata
- Milà chair
- Swatch
- Zara
- Yves Rocher
- S.S.S.S. stool by Philippe Starck

Chapter Seven: Tourist Spots in Paris

As mentioned earlier, it is truly an injustice for you and your whole being to not see Paris at least once in your lifetime! Call it extreme, but this city is genuinely one of the greatest places this world can offer. When you get here, it will feel like heaven on earth! For some it's one of the greatest experiences in their life, for others it is remarkably life – changing in many aspects, but at the end of the day, visiting Paris will be one of the greatest memories you could look back on and reminisce about. In this chapter, we'll give you ten of the best tourist spots and landmarks that you should not dare miss when you travel to the city of love.

1. The Eiffel Tower (La Tour Eiffel)

First stop, the very monument that defines the whole country of France! Paris will not be Paris if not for the magnificent Eiffel Tower. If for any reason, you only have a limited time, or a limited budget, or you just won a bet and you are only required to choose one destination in this city, then this is THE landmark to see! When you think about Paris, you think about the Eiffel Tower, and once you see it, I'm sure you'll never be the same person again. No doubt.

Why do you need to see this monumental monument? There are lots of reasons, but I don't want to bore you with history, so I'll just give you the awesome quick facts – the essential knowledge you need to know to truly appreciate this 'iron lady' that stood the test of time, and the reasons on why you should definitely see this monument with your own two eyes!

The Eiffel Tower Quick Facts

Location and Description:

The Eiffel Tower can be found in Champ de Mars in the city of Paris. It is also known as *La Dame de Fer* (Iron Lady). The tower was named after Gustave Eiffel, and it was originally built as the arch entrance during the 1889 World Fair.

It stands at about 1,050 feet tall or 320 meters, weighs 10,000 tons and it is made out entirely of iron. It is the tallest man made structure for over 41 years, before the World Trade Center in New York was built, and now has been surpassed by the Chrysler building also located in New York.

Interesting Fun Facts:

- Many people criticized the bold design of the Eiffel Tower back in the day.

- 250 million tourists have visited the tower since it's opening in 1889. Around 7 million people go here annually on average.

- Tourists can climb the stairs up to the second floor, and they can also reach the highest point through an elevator.

- Gustave Eiffel also built a small apartment at the upper portion of the tower. In 2016, a vacation rental company built a temporary apartment and held a contest so that they can spend a night on top of the Eiffel Tower.

- The names of the 72 French scientists are etched on the four sides of the tower.

- The Eiffel Tower had been recreated many times around the world in places such as Las Vegas, and Japan. It has also appeared in many movies and television shows ever since its erection.

2. Louvre Museum and Pyramid

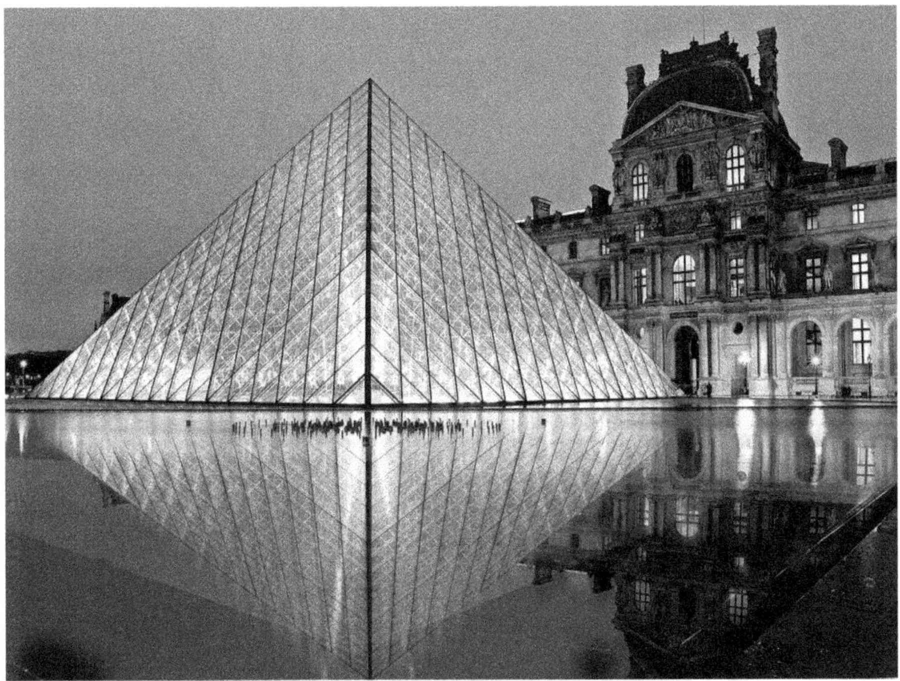

The next landmark you should see in Paris is the famous Louvre Museum; it wouldn't be hard to spot around town once you see the Louvre Pyramid in all its glory. This is not just a typical European museum. This is THE largest museum, and also one of the oldest on Earth! It houses the world – renowned painting of all time – the Mona Lisa. If you happen to saw the film called the Da Vinci Code, you can see the magnificent appearance of the Louvre Pyramid and museum in many scenes that matches the awesome performance of Tom Hanks. This is the classic, glamorous, and Parisian version of Egypt's Pyramid of Giza. It may not be one of the 7 wonders of the world, but it is definitely No. 1 in the world of art and history.

Here are some interesting fun facts about the Louvre Museum and the reasons why you should also put it in your bucket list especially if you're a history buff and an artist:

The Louvre Museum Quick Facts

Location and Description:

The Louvre Pyramid and Museum is located in the 1st arrondissement in central Paris, near the romantic Seine River. The pyramid is made out of about 700 glass panes, and stands at about 20 meters with an area of 1,225 square meters.

The museum was originally built around the 12th century, and served as a fortress to protect Parisians from Viking attacks. During the French Revolution in 1793, it then became a museum.

Interesting Fun Facts:

- The Louvre Museum is the most visited museum in Europe. There are about an average of 8 million tourists who visits this place yearly.

- It contains more than 35,000 items (paintings, sculptures, antiques, collections, and other works of art. There are around 6,700 paintings (66% from French artists) in total.

- It would take more than 100 days (almost 4 months) for you to see every single piece of art and collection.

- The works of several notable painters such as Leonardo da Vinci, Michelangelo, Raphael, Pablo Picasso, and Caravaggio are all housed in this museum.

- The ancient Greek statue of goddess Aphrodite called *Venus de Milo* can also be found here. You can also find about 50,000 ancient collections from Egypt in the Louvre Museum.

- During World War II, Nazi's used the museum as a storeroom for all the works of art they stole.

- The Louvre Museum is also said to be haunted by a mummy named Belphegor (yikes!).

3. *Notre Dame Cathedral (Notre Dame de Paris)*

Much like other countries in Europe, France is pretty much a solid Catholic country. Once you see their staggering cathedrals, you'd almost feel like it houses the Pope. Out of all the basilicas located in Paris, the Notre Dame Cathedral is the one that stood out because of its history, and architecture. It is also one of the largest religious buildings in the world. It's an institution built upon faith and devotion of the people. If you don't like going to church, seeing the cathedral will make you want to go to church!

Here are some interesting fun facts about the Notre Dame Cathedral and the reasons why it is every religious person's dream to go here and worship:

The Notre Dame Cathedral Quick Facts

Location and Description:

The cathedral of Notre Dame is located in the heart of Paris at the Ile de la Cite. Its proper name is Notre Dame de Paris or Our Lady of Paris. The grandiose architectural structure was built by many architects and engineers, as well as artists and sculptors from 1163 up to 1345. It was constructed for 182 years long!

The building is about 140 feet wide, and 400 feet in length. It's 'twin towers' are 200 feet with about 387 steps from the ground floor up to the highest level of the towers. It is also known as "The Forest," because during its construction there are approximately 1,300 trees used, even if it is built out of stone.

Interesting Fun Facts:

- The Notre Dame Cathedral is the site of the most important religious activities and ceremonies in France.

- It's almost twice as many visitors than the Eiffel Tower, with about 13 million visitors annually.

- Its roof is made out of 1,000 lead tiles, and the designers of the building introduced a new innovative architectural element called the flying buttresses.

- It is home to one of Europe's largest organs, and several musical instruments. The cathedral also has a lot of huge and heaviest church bells in the world, one of which is the bell located in the south tower that weighs about 13 tons.

- The Crown of Thorns (one of the most important religious artifacts in the world) is kept in the cathedral, and every year ceremonial events take place to venerate it.

- The classic book of Victor Hugo called 'The Hunchback of Notre Dame' was done to appreciate the cathedral, and increase its popularity.

- Famous French wire – walker Philippe Petit, crossed the twin towers of the Notre Dame Cathedral.

4. Seine River

If you visited the world famous Seine River, you will definitely fall in love with the place because of its serene yet spectacular scenery. The horizon, the clear waters, the cruises, the river side, the lovers and the whole ambience of the place will surely bring out the romantic side of you.

Famous for being the one of the hotspots for couples, the Seine River has more than 30 bridges that connect the city of Paris; the water is steady and very easy to navigate. It is very famous among tourists who wanted to cruise the city of Paris. The Seine River is truly one of Paris' must – see!

Here are some interesting fun facts about the Seine River and the reasons why couples and families love cruising the river to tour around Paris in a different way:

The Seine River Quick Facts

Location and Description:

The Seine River stretches in the whole city of Paris; it is linked to the River Rhine, and River Marne as well as the waterways in Belgium. The Seine River has an area of 30,000 square miles. Many bridges such as Pont Louis-Philippe, Pont Neuf, and Pont Des Arts are built over the river.

Interesting Fun Facts:

- The ashes of the famous French saint Joan of Arc are scattered in the Seine River specifically in Seine at Rouen.

- The river served as an inspiration for many world famous French painters and artists such as Alfred Sisley Henri Matisse, Raoul Dufy, and Claude Monet.

- Its main stream is the Oise River, the Eue River, the Aube River, and the Marne River.

- The quality of the river has dramatically improved over the years, it is now quite potable, and fishes such as the Atlantic salmon returned back to the river.

- The Seine River is also used as a cooling source for power stations in Paris.

- The most important artworks in history are kept underground, so whenever the Seine River will overflow, or if there is a forecast of flood, the artworks are moved to a higher facility.

5. Sacre Coeur Basilica

Another important landmark you should go to especially if you are a Catholic is called the Sacre Coeur Basilica, otherwise known as the Basilica of the Sacred Heart of Paris. This minor basilica is dedicated for the Sacred Heart of Jesus. The thing that makes this basilica iconic aside from its marvelous architecture and structure is its strategic location. It is the on top of a hill, the second highest point in the city of Paris. Lots of pilgrimage and catholic gatherings happens every year. Catholic tourists, and non – Catholics alike flock to this place to worship and pay respects.

Here are some interesting fun facts about the Sacre Coeur Basilica and the reasons why devoted and religious people love to spend time in the 'house of God':

The Sacre Coeur Basilica Quick Facts

Location and Description:

It is located in the summit of Montmartre Paris, erected on top of the hill, which is the second highest point in the city after the Eiffel Tower.

The Sacre Coeur Basilica stands at about 280 feet in length, 115 feet wide, and 272 feet in height. The basilica is the second famous religious institution in Paris next to Notre Dame. It also houses one of the heaviest church bells in the world (weighs about 21 tons) called the Savoyarde.

Interesting Fun Facts:

- The bronze statue of Joan of Arc and King Saint Louis IX is erected in the triple – arched portico of the basilica. The statues were designed by the famous Hippolyte Lefebvre.

- The interior of the basilica was created by Paul Abadie. It was inspired by the architectural style of the Romano – Byzantine period which gives the church a sense of peace and atmosphere of harmony.

- Its construction was from 1875 until 1914. The basilica was then sanctified after World War I in 1919.

- The style of the church was inspired from the Saint Sofia church in Constantinople, and the San Marco Cathedral in Venice Italy.

- The top of the dome of the church offers a phenomenal panoramic view of Paris. Fortunately it is open to tourists and locals alike.

- There are about an average of 11 million visitors annually (tourists, locals and pilgrims combined).

- The church site had been a sacred site especially during the time of the pagans. People called Druids worshipped in the summit, and ancient Romans are thought to have built temples for the gods (Mars and Mercury)

- The Sacre Coeur Basilica serves a double monument – it is both cultural and political. The popular vision of Jesus Christ in the basilica is that of a sympathetic and loving Christ.

6. Château de Versailles (Palace of Versailles)

Ever wondered what's it like to live as a King or Queen and be one of them royals? Well wonder no more! One of the most elegant and exquisite royal palaces in the world is open for tourists and natives alike. The Palace of Versailles will surely bring your royal fantasies to reality! Inside this splendid palace you will get to see the large rooms, halls, and gardens that are mostly covered in gold! If Mida was here, his golden touch will be nothing compared to the amount of gold used to build this place. In today's money, it will cost over $2 billion to build a palace like this.

What are you waiting for? Royal up and start living like a King!

Here are some interesting fun facts about the Château de Versailles and the reasons why you should check this place out while you are in Paris:

The Château de Versailles Quick Facts

Location and Description:

The Château de Versailles can be found in the South West region of France in *Ile de France.* The palace was originally built in the 1600's for King Louis XIV. It took more than 3000 people to construct the palace from the ground up. It is consisted of approximately 700 rooms, with roughly 1,200 fireplaces, and covers about 30,000 acres of land. The palace was the house of the French government for over 100 years starting in 1682 until 1789, when the French revolution began.

Interesting Fun Facts:

- The garden inside the Palace of Versailles has over 400 sculptures and approximately 1,400 fountains.

- There are about 6,000 paintings inside the palace, with over 5,000 pieces of items including furniture.

- Within the Palace of Versailles, there are other two smaller palaces called the Petit Trianon.

- During the time of King Louis XIV, there are almost 200 servants. The King of France also made everything a ceremony from the moment he wakes up until he goes to sleep (entitlement at its best!)

- The most interesting room inside the Palace is called the Hall of Mirrors, where around 3,000 candles were originally lighted up during King Louis XIV's time. It is also where the Treaty of Versailles was signed that ended World War I in 1919.

- Château de Versailles is where the French Revolution began ironically it is also where the place where the wars had ended.

- There are about an average of 5 million tourists yearly that wander around the grand halls of the palace, and about 10 million people walk in the gardens of Versaillles.

7. Pantheon

The Pantheon in Paris is no match compare to the ancient and authentic Pantheons of Greece; however, it is still one of the greatest landmarks you should visit while you are in the city. This is the French version of the house of gods inspired of course from the legendary Greek and Roman mythology. Its magnificent pillars and massive halls as well as its intricate architectural design will surely capture your attention, and make you pay homage to the Gods above. If you are a fan of literature, this will surely be a treat!

Here are some interesting fun facts about the Pantheon in Paris and the reasons why you should check this place out the "house of Gods":

The Pantheon Quick Facts

Location and Description:

It is located in Place du Panthéon Latin Quarter of Paris in the 5th arrondissement, and the building is over 272 feet tall. The Pantheon in Paris is from inspired from the Pantheon in Rome which means "every god."

The structure was originally built as a church dedicated to St. Genevieve, but today it is both used for religious functions and also as a burial place. The architect of the Pantheon in Paris is Jacques – Germain Soufflot. Unfortunately, Soufflot did not witness his final masterpiece because he died before the Pantheon's completion. Nevertheless, the Pantheon became one of the greatest architectural buildings in the 18th century and it is also the first ever monument built in Paris during the Neoclassicism era.

Interesting Fun Facts:

- The Pantheon took about 34 years to build from 1757 to 1791.

- It is about 85 meters wide and approximately 110 meters long.

- The monument is made out of marble and store

- It was built during the time of King Louis XV.

- Architect Guillaume Rondelet picked up where Jacques – Germain Soufflot left off and finished the building.

- In 1851, the Foucault's pendulum experiment was held at the famous Pantheon of Paris.

- Today lots of tourists and visitors from around the world go here every day. It is now a mausoleum.

8. L'Hotel National des Invalides

The National Residents of the Invalids is a feast for all the history buffs out there especially the admirers of General Napoleon Bonaparte, simply because this is where he was buried! Somewhere in this building lie the remains of one of the greatest and most brilliant military mind in history. Napoleon Bonaparte led the stabilization of the French Republic, and had won many battles for France. His military feats were revolutionary, and although he had already fallen, history will always remember him as one of the most significant and notable leaders of the 19th century.

Here are some interesting fun facts about the L'Hotel National des Invalides and the reasons why this is one of the liberating places in Paris:

The L'Hotel National des Invalides Quick Facts

Location and Description:

The National Residents of the Invalids is located at the Seine River (left bank) across Alexandre III Bridge near the Esplanade des Invalides, if you're coming from Champs – Elysees.

The site began construction in 1670 and was done after 6 years, around 1676. It was originally built as a military hospital for the French military soldiers who were wounded and poor. It was constructed during the reign of the King of the Sun (King Louis XIV).

Interesting Fun Facts:

- During the battle in Bastille, 28,000 weapons stored in the Invalides were stolen by the crowd.

- The tomb of Napoleon Bonaparte was designed by Visconti, and the Invalides received the general's dead body on December 15 1840. On 1861, Bonaparte finally came to his resting place inside a crypt under the dome in the National Residents of the Invalids.

- The St. Louis des Invalides church (also part of the landmark) and the golden dome were created by Jules Mansart, and were later finished around 1708 by Robert de Cotte. The Esplanade des Invalides was also designed by De Cotte.

- The church of Invalides covers about 13 hectares, and it was regarded as a classic masterpiece in French architecture.

- Today there are other structure and museums built around this landmark such as the Musée de l'Ordre de la Libération, Musée de l'Armée, Musée des Plans-Reliefs, and L'Eglise de St-Louis-des-Invalides.

9. Élysée Palace

The Elysee Palace is the White House version of France. This is where the president of France resides, and since 1871, it has been the formal residence of the French Republic. Obviously, this security here is tight, but fortunately the Elysee Palace is still open to tourists at least once a year, around the 3rd week of September during the *Journées du Patrimoine* day. Be sure to arrive early for you to avoid long lines. The gates of the palace open at 9 AM. This is where the French government holds its official meetings, political parties come and go, and lots of presidents from different countries have been here to meet with the French President.

The L'Hotel National des Invalides Quick Facts

Location and Description:

The Elysee Palace's main entrance is in #55 Rue du Faubourg-St-Honoré. The palace opens unto the **Cour d'Honneur**, and it is also parallel to Avenue des Champs-Elysées. The building has two wings. It is one of the most prestigious and coveted palace in Paris. All the rooms overlook the Parc de l'Elysée.

Interesting Fun Facts:

- Salon Murat is the most famous room in the palace, and it housed the Council of Ministers since the time of President Pompidou

- Meetings in Salon Murat are scheduled every Wednesday, where the President and Prime Minister of France meet.

- The room was originally built for Napoleon I's brother – in – law, Joachim Murat.

- Another famous room is the Salon Pompadour. It served as the bedchamber of Napoleon I, and was also the former state bedroom of Marquise de Pompadour.

- The room is covered with 17th century tapestries and furnishings inspired by Louis XV and XVI. The president used this room to grant audience to his guests.

10. Arc de Triomphe

The last landmark in this list is definitely not the least! It's the finale, the cherry on top that will complete your trip to Paris. Similar to the Eiffel Tower, the Arc de Triomphe (Arch of Triumph) also defines what Paris is all about, what it had gone through, and a reminder of what it can become. This famous monument is a symbol of a feat achieved during the time of French Emperor Napoleon around 1806. It was originally built as a tribute, and in honor of the French army called the Grand Armee for winning many battles, and conquering most of Europe. Salute to the French troops!

The Arc de Triomphe Quick Facts

Location and Description:

The Arc of Triumph is situated in the middle of 12 avenues in Paris. The monument is 162 feet tall, 72 feet deep and 150 feet wide. There are two vaults; the smaller vault measures about 62 feet tall, while the original vault is 95.8 feet tall and 48 feet wide. It was the largest triumphal arch throughout history until 1982 when North Korea built one that is just slightly bigger.

The architects of this arch are Jean Chalgrin, and Jean Huyot. The construction costs over 9.3 million francs, which was a huge amount at the time. Unfortunately Napoleon did not live to see the finished monument, but he built a wooden model back in 1810, possibly a wooden replica of it, so that he can go through the arch when he returned to Paris with his wife.

Interesting Fun Facts:

- Fighter pilot Charles Godefroy flew his plane through the Arc de Triomphe in honor of the pilots killed during World War I.

- There were two assassination attempts at the arch against World War Generals Charles de Gaulle and Jacques Chirac. Fortunately both men survived.

- The Arch of Triumph has a memorial flame that's been burning non-stop since 1923.

- The Germans in 1871 and the Nazi's during World War II marched underneath the Arc de Triomphe as an insult to France.

- Since the Arc de Triomphe was a symbol of French victories, the French marched through it after World War I ended in 1919 and after World War II this time with the Allies in 1944 and1945.

- France's Tomb of the Unknown Soldier lies under the Arc de Triomphe. It was placed there on November 10, 1920 with the inscription above it reading:
  "Here lies a French soldier who died for his Fatherland 1914 -1918."

Chapter Eight: Interacting with Paris

If the different tourist attractions are not enough for you, then maybe you need a little more adventure and immersion to truly appreciate what Paris has to offer. One way of doing that is by interacting not only with its places but also the people and culture embedded within.

In this chapter, we have put together 10 of the best things you need to try and do while you are in Paris. Some of these places are also great tourist destinations wherein you can enjoy and get to know the people, the culture and Paris' way of life through the eyes of a local. You'll then discover why the art in Paris is truly a state – of – the – art in itself.

1. *Opéra National de Paris - Palais Garnier*

The *Opera National de Paris* or simply known as the Opera Garnier is one of the most famous opera houses in the world. The whole architectural structure of the building is magnanimous and magnificent in every way. You'd think that the stage or the theatre proper is the only elegant – looking part in the whole opera house just like in most theatres, but for the Opera Garnier, it's halls, and staircases is actually much grandiose than the actual stage itself. This architectural feat was built under Napoleon III by Architect Charles Garnier in 1861. Its original name before was Salle des Capucines but the name Palais Garnier stuck with it.

Interesting Fun Facts:

- The Palais Garnier's grand staircase was designed for people watching. Once you are in the staircase or in one of the balconies, you will be force to gaze down at the people below or across you.

- The staircase is also shallow because it was designed to prevent women (back in the day) from showing their ankles (talk about being too conservative).

- The Opera Garnier was surrounded by lots of banks because the aristocrats and rich people of France wanted to show off their new jewels that they have picked up from the banks prior to going at the theatre. Lots of banks are still open today around the area.

- The top tier of the opera house is called the Chicken Coup. The origin story of how the name came about is when the middle class people started bringing their own food inside the theater because they can't afford to buy the expensive foods inside the theater. They then started throwing food from the top tier if they saw a popular actor that they don't like. The vendors outside started selling tomatoes and apples for this very purpose.

- The famous musical of all time – The Phantom of the Opera was inspired by the flooded basement of the the Opera Garnier. The workers in 1861 discovered cellars and an underground lake directly beneath the building because of this, writer Gaston Leroux got inspired from the discovery and led to him writing the story of the Phantom of the Opera in 1910.

- The Opera Garnier or Palais Garnier is home to many ballet, and theatrical performances in the Europe.

- The Opera House has a 1,979 seating capacity, and it is located in Rue Scribe in Paris.

2. Moulin Rouge Theater

Paris is widely known for being the cabaret capital of the world. If you are fond of musicals, then you should definitely check out the world famous Moulin Rouge. There are about 600,000 visitors that watch the Moulin Rouge annually. It is over 100 years old already, and it became a Parisian institution that every musical fan need to experience! It is located in the 18th district, and has become a symbol of the bohemian culture in Paris. The Moulin Rouge is made up of the most colorful costumes, and it is also has the most exquisite dances and story in theatre history.

Interesting Fun Facts:

- The Moulin Rouge began in 1889 which was the same year the Eiffel Tower was officially unveiled to the public.

- The Moulin Rouge cabaret was originally dedicated to the women, the dance and the cancan. Moulin Rouge (Le Premier Palais des Femmes) was known as the First Women Palace, because lots of beautiful women dancer in France was included in the show. It was started by Joseph Oller and Charles Zidler who were Spanish businessmen.

- The dances of Moulin Rouge is iconic especially the moves called 'quadrille' or French Cancan which involves the women doing high kicks while wearing gorgeously flowing skirts

- The Moulin Rouge Theater has only a 900 seating capacity, but it has been operational for almost 125 years already.

- The cost of the show is about 100 Euros, but it's definitely a worthy experience.

3. Musée d'Art moderne de la Ville de Paris

The Musee d'Art Moderne de la Ville de Paris is being visited by about 800,000 tourists annually. It was established in 1937, and it was one of the best and most famous art museums in the city.

The Musee d'Art Moderne de la Ville de Paris houses the some of the best collections of notable French artists, from painters to sculptors, to architects, designers, and the likes. Their works are displayed through an exhibit. This museum is a government institution wherein you can enjoy guided tours, lectures, interactive exhibits, and it also has various activities for kids and families. There are also lots of restaurants and food stalls around the area.

Here are some of the famous artists, whose works are displayed in different kinds of exhibits inside the museum, make sure to browse them all:

- Pablo Picasso
- Henri Matisse
- Raoul Dufy
- Maurice de Vlaminck
- Georges Rouault
- Fernand Léger
- Georges Braque
- Francis Picabia
- Amedeo Modigliani
- Giorgio de Chirico
- Kees van Dongen
- Pierre Bonnard
- Chaïm Soutine
- Nam June Paik
- John Heartfield
- André Derain
- Suzanne Valadon
- Pierre Soulages
- Maurice Utrillo
- Robert and Sonia Delaunay
- Frantiek Kupka
- Yves Klein
- Juan Gris
- Hans Bellmer
- René Iché
- Jean Fautrier
- Wolf Vostell

- Jean Arp
- Alberto Giacomett

4. Jardin des Tuileries

The Jardin des Tuileries or simply known as the Tuileries Gardens is the largest park in the city. It is also one of the oldest gardens in France. The garden's astounding landscapes, panoramic view, and rich history is what makes it one of the most popular tourist destinations of tourists and Parisian alike. The Garden of Tuileries offers a great view of the Louvre Museum, the Champs – Elysees Avenue as well as the Arch of Triumph. This place also has interactive arcades at night, where you and your family can hang out and enjoy – not to mention, the London like Ferris wheel situated on it.

Interesting Fun Facts:

- The meaning of Tuileries is tiles. The palace and the garden of Tuileries were built around 1560's after Henri II's death. His widow, Catherine de Medicis ordered to build a Palais de Tuileries because at that time the area where it was built was composed of clay quarry for tiles.

- Catherine de Medicis wanted to build a garden inspired from her native roots in Tuscany Italy.

- Around 1660 up to 1664, the garden had some major renovations by French designer André Le Nôtre. He was the most notable garden architect during the Sun King's time; he was also the one who designed the garden in the Palace of Versailles.

- The garden had been open to the public since the 18th century making it one of the first parks to offer the same amenities most parks have today such as kiosks, cafes, chairs, desks, and public toilets. French families and friends had gone here throughout the ages.

- The garden also houses two museums; the Galerie Nationale du Jeu de Paume and the Musée de l'Orangerie which contains tons of paintings and sculptures including Cluade Monet's famous water lily paintings.

5. Maison européenne de la photographie

Paris is easily one of the best places to photograph because it is just naturally photogenic! This is perhaps also the reason why the world – renowned photographers and artists in the world came from Paris. It has become a natural inclination for natives to appreciate their city's beauty by either painting it, or in this case taking a world – class photograph so that people will be reminded of not just the scenery but also the stories behind each picture.

The Maison européenne de la photographie pays tribute to Paris' world famous photographers. According to historians, French photographers have been in love with the City of Light which is why many of them made Paris and its people their most favorite subject. It is located next to St. Paul Metro Station, at Rue de Fourcy and the site is also near the Seine River. This is the best place to see if you are into visual arts.

Interesting Fun Facts:

- The Maison européenne de la photographie contains the biggest collections of photographs not just in Paris or in France but the whole European continent

- Three types of visual arts are exhibited and displayed in the museum; the photographs, the printed page, and video reels.

- The façade of the building as well as its staircase are all from the classical era of architecture.

- The museum has several facilities including an auditorium, huge library, and a viewing room that contains the widest selection of films in Europe.

- There are tons of exhibitions, events, and conferences every year in the MEP.

- The museum also houses conservation workshops, and photographic restorations.

- There are about 20,000 works of art including silver and digital photography as well as videos that are of rare editions and collector's items.

- The collection of the photographs and videos is dedicated to the contemporary creation.

- It is currently directed by Jean-Luc Monterosso since 1996.

6. Centre de Création Artistique

You will never run out of historical art museums to see in Paris, the best part about it is they never run out of artworks to display! If you think you had enough of gazing at paintings, and looking at beautiful photographs, but still wanted to learn more about Paris' culture, then you need to head to the Cent Quatre, also known as Centre de Création Artistique. This is where all kinds of artists collide. From painters, to sculptors, to modern era photographers, dancers, filmographers, actors and writers you can find them here in one place, prepare to hang out with people with the same interests, same passion, and same vision and together advance the artistic endeavors forward.

Interesting Fun Facts:

- Cent Quatre (which means 104) is located in #104 Rue d'Aubervilliers. It is the cultural center of the city and had been open to the public since October 2008 (from its former place in the 19th arrondissement.

- Artists of all disciplines are invited here to work in various projects while using the studios on the site, and allowing their works to be seen by the public during production.

- The Centre de Création Artistique constantly held different contemporary art exhibitions, and it is also the hub of young Parisians who were into urban dancing, or audiovisual artistry.

- Entrepreneurs are also welcome here because the center fosters a business incubator for social and cultural endeavors.

- The Cent Quatre has an area of about 15,800 square meters, and there are about 25,000 square meters of space that is used by the artists during production and exhibitions.

7. Grand Musée du Parfum

Only in Paris can you find a museum dedicated to nothing but perfumes and fragrance! This is truly the city where art meets glamour. The place is just a newly opened museum, and it contains not just the latest perfumes today but also has a collection of fragrances from around the world, some of it from many centuries ago. This is the first ever museum dedicated for the art of fragrance in Europe and perhaps in the world, so if you are in anyway interested and curious about how the aristocrats and ancient people roll back in the day, then look no further and let the Grand Musée du Parfum take you back one scent at a time!

The mansion museum is located in Rue du Faubourg Saint-Honoré and it just opened this year. Ironically France is still the leading and biggest exporter of fragrance in the world. Prepare to unlock your imagination, and discover the olfactory mysteries of the human sense. The scent of Paris will surely make your trip a memorable one.

Interesting Fun Facts:

- Guillaume de Maussion was the co-founder and first director of the fragrance museum. He is an entrepreneur, a pioneer and an expert in the French perfume industry.

- The museum features the latest and high-tech graphic, video and sound installations to make the multi-sensory journey an awesome educational experience.

- You will learn the history as well as the art and science of scent and perfume making.
- You can also smell the first fragrance ever created by mankind in Ancient Egypt called the Kyphi which was made out of a pungent woody compound used to invoke the Gods.
- You can also find another artistic marvel within the museum called the Garden of Scents where you can learn the importance of the sense of smell and how it is linked to human emotions.
- State-of-the-art technology means that visitors can record the fragrance accents which they can also purchase right on the spot.

8. Parc zoologique de Thoiry

If you have children or you simply want to escape the hustle and bustle of the Paris' world of art and architecture, then take a breather in the Parc zoologique de Thoiry. The Thoiry Safari Park is a very interesting zoo because the animals are free to roam across 8 kilometers of land! You can actually interact with over 800 animals while you are riding on your own vehicle. Not only will you get to be with these animals, but you can also have a liberating time alone in this great safari. If you are into zoology, an environmentalist, or you simply just wanted to have experience Paris in a whole new non-artistic way, then head over to Parc zoologique de Thoiry and enjoy with your family.

Interesting Fun Facts:

- Part of the tour can be done on foot in the zoological and botanical gardens where you can see the first Komodo dragons living in France

- Visitors can walk amongst the lions in a glass tunnel, and have an awesome adventure trail in the 'Île Mystérieuse' (Mysterious Island)

- The gardens inside the zoo occupies 95 hectares of the site and have been laid out in former woodland of beech, oak, hornbeam, and chestnut trees

- You can also visit the Château de Thoiry which was originally designed as a solar calendar

- The main hall of the park is built with the same proportions as the royal burial chamber in the Great Pyramid of Giza called the Pythagorean triangles. It is the pivot of a solar calendar for which the horizon is the dial and the views are the hands

9. Cité de l'Architecture & du Patrimoine

For all the architects, engineers, sculptors, and people who are interested in facades and pillars out there, this is the museum for you! The Cité de l'Architecture & du Patrimoine is made out of 1,000 years of architectural creations, so prepare your construction hats and watch out there might be ancient falling debris around!

The museum is located in Palais de Chaillot just across the Eiffel Tower's site. The building measures about 8,000 square meters, and it is a labor of love from French architects in Paris.

Interesting Fun Facts:

- The Cité de l'Architecture & du Patrimoine offer visitors an experience through the rich architectural heritage of France starting from the Middle Ages to the present day.

- Life-size productions and replica are reproduced such as the doorway of Chartres cathedral, the painted cupola of the cathedral of Cahors and an apartment from Corbusier's 'Cité radieuse.'

- Diverse temporary exhibitions (monographs of architects, exhibitions relating to current themes, exhibition workshops for children, etc.) focus on history or the challenges of today.

10. Jardin du Luxembourg

If you truly wanted to interact with Paris in all aspects; the art, the history, the architecture, the culture, the heritage, the class, and the people then the ultimate Garden of Luxembourg is the place to be. The Jardin du Luxembourg is without a doubt the best park in Paris, it is located between the Saint-Germain-des-Prés and the Latin Quarter. This is where nature meets history!

Interesting Fun Facts:

- Commissioned by Queen Marie de Medici, the Garden of Luxembourg is inspired by the Boboli Gardens in Florence, and it was finished in 1612.
- The whole garden covers 25 hectares of land; it has a French garden and an English garden.
- There's a forest, and an orchard as well as a large pond.
- There are about 106 statues including the legendary Medici fountain, the Orangerie and the Pavillon Davioud.
- There are also lots of fun activities for kids and families including the rides, slides and even remote control boats. People also play chess and tennis inside the park.

- The Garden of Luxemborg also holds various cultural shows and exhibits as well as concerts from time to time.

Chapter Nine: Nightlife in Paris

Another best way to experience Paris is during night time. Paris offers a variety of choices on how to enjoy the night life that aren't just limited in going to clubs or bars. You can have lots of options where you can relax, enjoy and have the best time with your family and loved ones. Night life in Paris is where you will see the city in a very different way! It is perhaps the only time where you will get to witness the true glow of the city of light, and the romantic side of the city of love. Here are 10 different ways on how you can spend the night in your stay in Paris, and the best districts you should go to at night. Party like a Parisian!

1. *Bastille*

Bastille isn't just the place where history was made; it's also the center of nightlife in Paris! Forget history, forget the art and whatnot, when the sun sets, and the night arrives, the once historically rich district will turn into one of the liveliest places in the city.

Metro Bastille has lots of nightclubs, mix and traditional cafes, dive bars, and music venues. You can start bar hopping from Rue de Lappe to Rue de la Roquette. The traditional Salsa and Marenge dancing is huge thing if you're going to go clubbing in Bastille. This is where French tradition meets the electrifying music of the 21st century.

The place is overcrowded almost every night, lots of people in their 20's, and young professionals are mostly the people who come here. You can surely meet the next generation of France if you decided to go out for a night with your friends. Who knows, you might meet the next Napoleon!

Here are some of the best bars and nightclubs in Bastille:

- **Sans Sanz**
  Location: 49 Rue du Faubourg St. Antoine
  Description: The club is famous for its young cosmopolitan crowd.

- **La Balajo**
  Location: 9 Rue de Lappe
  Description: Has a reputation for salsa nights

- **La Mécanique Ondulatoire**
  Location: Passage Thiere
  Description: Known as the top party place for rockers in Paris, and offers 3 levels of activity.

2. *Oberkampf*

Before Bastille became the nightlife center in the city of lights, Oberkampf is the coolest district to go to especially during the 90's, and continues to be one of the best places to spend your night while you are in Paris.

The people who usually go here are mostly young and chic Parisians. The district had a bit of bad reputation over the years because of its occasional rowdiness. This is also the hub of hipsters, and the place offers the most interesting clubs, bars, and restaurants in the city.

Here are some of the best bars and nightclubs in Oberkampf:

- **Café Charbon**
  Location: 109 Rue Oberkampf
  Description: Hipsters Best Choice. It has an old-style décor, and lively night bar.

- **Au Chat Noir**
  Location: Rue Oberkampf
  Description: cozy café, perfect for young professionals. The place is quite elegant; mostly offer cocktails and wines at night.

- **L'Alimentation Generale**
  Location: 109 rue Oberkampf
  Description: So – called "grocery store," you can literally buy cupboards, supplies etc. Offers a variety of beers, and has a large space where you can enjoy dancing to the DJ's beat.

- **UFO Bar**
  Location: 49, rue Jean-Pierre Timbaud
  Description: Bars perfect for rockers and punks out there. The place is painted in red, has lots of rock band posters, and vintage comic book collections.

3. Ménilmontant and Gambetta

This district is one of the hidden facets of nightlife in Paris. It is located between Rue Oberkampf, and Belleville. If you seriously wanted to just go partying with your friends away from lots of tourists, then this place is a great 'hideout.'

The district is full of bars that are cheap, lively, and it touches the 11th and 20th arrondissement in Paris. This district is also the hub or indi – punk rockers as well as musicians. It offers a mix of bars, night clubs, cafes, and also holds lots of exhibits, mini concerts (local and international startup bands), theatrical renditions as well as different film screenings.

Here are some of the best bars and nightclubs in Ménilmontant and Gambetta:

- **La Bellevilloise**

  Location: 19 -21 Rue Boyer

  Description: It simultaneously a bar, club, exhibition space, and a club. Perfect for people born in the 80's and artists alike because there's an 80's night on the basement level, while a film screening night on top. It also holds various music festivals.

- **La Maroquinerie**

  Location: 23 Rue Boyer

  Description: Hub of musicians, this is where live bands go to, and is popular for Indie Club nights.

- **La Flèche d'Or Bar and Concert Venue**

  Location: East Paris

  Description: Popular for being the Indie – rock temple bar in the district.

4. The Marais

If you have read throughout this book, the district of Marais is often mentioned either for the best accommodation areas, food and shopping district, and tourist spots. What makes this district more dynamic is because it is the place to be if you're looking for diversity and equality – at night in Paris.

This is the hub of the LGBT community; it's also famous for being one of the beloved spots in Paris because everyone is welcome here with no judgment whatsoever. Check out the bars and clubs on the next section.

Here are some of the best bars and nightclubs in Le Marais:

- **Amnesia**
  Location: 42 Rue Vielle du Temple
  Description: Hub for gays mostly. Offers disco, bar mixing, funk, and soul music genres.

- **3W Café**
  Location: 8 Rue des Ecouffes
  Description: Known for being a lesbian bar, offers coffee, beers, and cocktails.

- **Andy Wahloo**
  Location: 69 Rue des Gravilliers
  Description: Hub for 'fashionistas,' and is a Moroccan – themed bar where people fight for the coveted "seats, "has lots of authentic and colorful artifacts and spice rack.

- **Stolly's**
  Location: 16 Rue Cloche - Perce
  Description: Mainly attracts Anglophone crowd. The place is not just a bar but also has a weird combination of entertainment setting.

5. *Belleville*

If you look at the photo above, this place sort of looks like a fine and quiet district, but at night it's bustling with Parisians looking to have a good time!

Another unchartered territory by tourists, famous for being the birth place of the great Edith Piaf. Belleville district is a middle class community, and it has been a hub for nightlife in Paris. The place also attracts a mixed crowd from youngsters, young professionals, gays and lesbians as well as middle age adults. It will surely give you and your friends a memorable night and an authentic experience. Check out the bars and clubs on the next section.

Here are some of the best bars and nightclubs in Belleville:

- **Aux Folies**
  Location: 8 Rue de Belleville
  Description: The most recommended place by Belleville locals and residents. It has flourescently lit interiors; the drinks are very cheap, although no food is served. The place also features movie marathons. It's fully – packed every night and on weekends.

- **La Java**
  Location: 105 Rue Faubourg du Temple
  Description: This place is famous for French musician Edith Piaf. This is where she started and made her debut in the music scene. Offers food and drinks as well as an eclectic mix of sounds

- **Okubi**
  Location: 219 Rue Saint-Maur
  Description: It is a lesbian bar, newly – opened but is one of the district's best new hotspots at night.

6. *Champs-Elysées*

Ah! The coveted and famous district of Paris – the Champs – Elysées! Not just famous for its luxurious hotels and shopping malls, but also famous for its nightlife. If you're tourists who have lots of money to splurge, you should definitely hang out in one of the bars and restaurants in Champs – Elysées at night. The place may not be recommended if you wanted to avoid lot of tourists and well Parisians alike. However if you'd like to party all night and hop from one bar to another, this is where you should go. The big – city experience of the high – end clubs will surely leave you wanting for more!

Here are some of the best bars and nightclubs in Champs – Elysées:

- **Le Queen**
  Location: 102 Avenue des Champs-Elysees
  Description: Primarily a gay bar, and offers a night of endless dancing and music. Different kinds of drink ranging from expensive beers, cool cocktails, and mojitos are also served.

- **Man Ray**
  Location: 34 Rue Marbeuf
  Description: This place is a crowd favorite and a hotspot for tourists especially for those who are fans of Johnny Depp and Sean Penn. They are the part owners of this club, and if you go here chances are you'll see them, a bit exclusive for the rich and famous.

- **Le Regine**
  Location: 49 Rue de Ponthieu
  Description: One of the most interesting clubs in the district! This bar is continuously revamping itself almost every night. Some nights it's a disco bar, some night its electro, perfectly suited for both the youngsters and young – at –hearts.

Another interesting thing about this bar is that every Thursday night if you're a guy, you can get in for free provided that you dressed up like a woman.

7. *Montmartre and Pigalle*

Pigalle is famously known as the seedy sex center of Paris. It has lots of cool bars and restaurants where you can hang out after watching the Moulin Rouge. The Montmartre is another great place to hang out at night because it offers a somewhat less gritty ambience. You can find the most diverse themes of bars and music in both districts.

Here are some of the best bars and nightclubs in Montmartre and Pigalle:

- **Divan du Monde**
  Location: Rue des Martyrs
  Description: It was previously called as Divan Japonais, once a historic site prized by famous Parisians like Henri Toulouse de Lautrec. Today it's one of the most dynamic bars in the district, offering different themes such as rock, hip-hop, goth, and live music.

- **Lux Bar**
  Location: 12 Rue Lepic
  Description: This place is a local favorite. This is where you can meet the residents of the district where you can drink and eat for less. Rockabilly music is what this bar is all about.

- **Au Rendez-Vous des Amis**
  Location: 23 Rue Gabrielle
  Description: This place is near the famous Sacre Coeur Basilica, which is why you can expect a toned – down version of this bar. There are no party happenings here but there's still a "happy hour" the café bar offers light drinks and it is

mostly a hub for students who are minor, and some locals.

8. *Grands Boulevards and Sentier*

The Grand Boulevard is located in the center of the 2nd arrondissement in Paris. It's ready – to – wear shops and boutiques by day are no match to its ready – to – party lifestyle at night! Lots of Parisians and tourists also come down to this place to spend the night hanging out with their friends. This is the friendliest place you could go into especially if you're still a student.

Here are some of the best bars and nightclubs in Grand Boulevard and Sentier:

- **La Conserverie**
  Location: 37 bis Rue de Sentier
  Description: The place is covered with nuit bleu décor, has a velvet sofa, and cheap beers as well as tasty cocktails and wines. You can literally just chill out here.

- **Silencio**
  Location: 142 Rue Montmartre
  Description: This place is exclusive and for members – only type of club. It's worth it to be a member though especially if you are an artist or into the media arts. The place is patterned after the film Mullholland Drive, and the part – owner of the club is famous director David Lynch. It usually features theatrical performances, movie marathons, exhibits, and it also has an art library, and reflective dance floor. It is only open until midnight.

9. St – Germain – des – Prés

Another coveted neighborhood probably next to Avenue des Champs – Elysees is St – Germain – des –Prés. Even if the right bank in Paris is the dead center of nightlife, people still come here to have a night full of fun and glamour. This is mostly a hub of students from the famous university in France the Sorbonne University. You can expect lots of students hanging out in this district, and also lots of tourists coming from nearby attractions. Get ready to splurge if you wanted to experience its night life!

Here are some of the best bars and nightclubs in St – Germain – des –Prés:

- **Coolin**

  Location: 15 Rue Clement

  Description: Europe's nightlife and probably western bars in general will not be complete without an Irish touch! Coolin is an Irish pub that offers a cool ambience, live music, and of course Guinness!

- **Les Etages**

  Location: 5 Rue de Buci

  Description: The interior of this bar is off the charts! It has lavish tile – mosaic tables, warm colors, and elegant lights. It is truly a refreshing way to chill out into the night after a long day. It also has a branch in Le Marais.

- **Chez Georges**

  Location: 11 Rue des Canettes

  Description: This place is known for being a "cave – bar," no clautrophobics allowed! This is a favorite hub of students, and locals because it is a cool place. You can play a game of chess, or dance your night away to pop music.

10. Place Vendome - Faubourg St-Honoré

The Place Vendome in Paris is home to the most lucrative bars and party places. If you wanted to be seen and heard, this is the perfect place for you. Get ready to spend lots of money, and be one of them celebrities! Famous people from Hollywood and even in Europe come to this district to spend and party the night away. This is a hub for the shopaholics and fashionistas in the city. You can find lots of

famous people around especially models, photographers, designers and entrepreneurs from the fashion scene.
Here are some of the best bars and nightclubs in Place Vendome - Faubourg St-Honoré:

- **Hotel Costes**
  Location: Faubourg St-Honoré
  Description: A crowd favorite, one of the most luxurious hotels in the district. This is a fashion set lounge that is highly recommended for its awesome cuisine and tasty before – dinner cocktails and drinks.

- **The Hemingway Bar**
  Location: 15 Place Vendome
  Description: It is named as the Hemingway Bar for one major reason: this is the place where famous French writer of all time Ernest Hemingway hangs out with other literary folks. It is still a world – renowned Ritz bar that provides a chic vibe perfectly suited for people who loves to dress up and have a toast. No cheapskate allowed!

Chapter Ten: Off - Beaten Path in Paris

"And I…I took the road less traveled by and that has made all the difference" (The Road Not Taken, Robert Frost. 1920)

Robert Frost in his poem The Road Not Taken says it best, and it is particularly true when it comes to travelling.

Paris is a place where you can find not just the city's popular tourist spots, but also the beautiful places that are usually not on every travel list. Sometimes though, the greatest experience comes from the most unexpected places. Try to go off the tracks this time, because in the end it's all going to be worth it. Here are top 10 off - beaten paths in Paris that you should try to discover for yourself so you can look at the 'city of light' from a different perspective.

1. Gaîté Lyrique

The La Gaîté Lyrique is not a typical museum, the structure is a remnant of classic baroque architecture in France, and this venue was also a former 19th century music hall. The exterior is of classic French style structure, but inside the museum it's nothing but art in the 21st century. The place is full of all kinds of modern art combined with the technologies of the digital age. It's perfect for creative artists and techy people alike. This is the place where classic art meets trendy technology.

Many events are being held in the museum such as interactive workshops for adults and kids, concerts, dance performances, exhibits and art fests. There is also a sort of futuristic library facility inside the museum, and video consoles are also on display. Not a lot of tourists and even artists know this place, so you can be sure to have a great time with your family and see how artists in today's world are incorporating technology to continue and further advance the artistic movement forward.

Here are the details of this off – beaten path:

Location: 3bis Rue Papin, 3rd arrondissement
Contact No.: +33 1 53 01 52 00
Nearest Metro station: Réaumur Sébastopol

2. *La Pagode*

Another great place that not a lot of tourists and locals know of is called La Pagode. It is an authentic Japanese pagoda that offers exclusive movie access in its movie theater. The interior of the pagoda have silk walls that are used as a screen room during the film showing. You will also notice the candelabras being held by golden dragons, and several paintings of Japanese warriors - truly a touch of Asian art in the heart of Europe. After the film you can enjoy the beautiful scenery while sipping an authentic ginseng tea and Japanese delicacies. The area has been given a cultural status by the government of Paris; it is truly a remarkable place you should go into to experience watching French films in a Japanese style setting.

Here are the details of this off – beaten path:

Location: 57 Bis Rue de Babylone, 7th arrondissement
Contact No.: +33 1 45 55 48 48
Nearest Metro Station: Saint-François-Xavier

3. Le Ballon de Paris

What do you think is better than actually going to the Eiffel Tower or Paris? The answer is flying above it! If you want to experience the city from a bird's eye view, then head over to Le Ballon de Paris! It's actually quite surprising that not a lot of tourists know you can hop on a hot air balloon, and see the entire city from a different perspective. So if you wanted to escape the overcrowded and claustrophobic atmosphere of the Eiffel Tower tour, then seeing it from above might be the best alternative for you. Only disclaimer is, it's obviously not for people who are afraid of heights!

The balloon can reach as high as 490 feet or about a 12 story building; it is anchored in Parc André Citroën, which is also a great park in itself. From up above you can see the entire city, feel the breeze, and see Parisians and their whereabouts. You'll be swinging with the wind in no time, and it will also feel like you've already capture everything Paris has to offer once you're up in the air. Try checking it out and fell in love with the whole city of Paris.

Here are the details of this off – beaten path:

Location: Parc André Citroën, 15th arrondissement
Contact No.: +33 1 44 26 20 00
Nearest Metro Station: Javel

4. Le Carreau du Temple

This cultural center is located near Le Marais but fortunately, there are not a lot of tourists that flock here. The main difference of this cultural center is that its location was actually central in French history especially during the time of the Templars and Crusades. It has a community – based feel and features tiny art galleries with the most diverse of themes it focuses on minimal things like shoes, dance, street – food, sports etc.

The Le Carreau du Temple also holds various events such as contemporary theater programs, art fests, and exhibits. The venue has a large space, because it was also a former lofty market hall. The cultural center is hotspot for serious French artists so if you wanted to meet people and learn from them and get to know why they are pursuing this passion, then come over to Le Carreau du Temple, they might bring out your artistic side.

Here are the details of this off – beaten path:

Location: 4 rue Eugène Spuller, 3rd arrondissement
Contact No.: +33 1 83 81 93 30
Nearest Metro Station: Temple

5. *Musée Rodin*

There aren't a lot of sculptors nowadays, so if you're one of them, then I salute you! You're one of the last in this world! You're basically an endangered species, and hopefully your masterpiece will be up there someday among the greatest sculptors of all time. If you're a sculptor, or just an extraordinary person who are interested in statues and the stories behind them, then you should definitely head over to Musée Rodin. This museum is solely dedicated to the greatest sculptor the world has ever known – Auguste Rodin. His name may not ring a bell for some, but his works of art over the years will surely make you bow down if one day you see him (in heaven probably).

His famous and world – renowned masterpieces include The Kiss, The Gates of Hell, The Burghers of Calais, and wait there's one more…it's the most popular piece of sculpted art in history. Let me think for a second…thinking…thinking…you're probably screaming right now. It's The Thinker!

His moving works truly deserves a statue in every corner of Paris, even if you're not into statues but for sure after you see Rodin's masterpiece, you'll probably be much interested than ever. His sculptures will ignite curiosity, and will make you really want to learn the stories behind it.

Auguste Rodin started drawing at the age of 10, and was admitted in art school at the age of 14. Lots of artists say he is too advanced for his age because he was already recognized very early on in his career.

In this museum, Rodin's works of art are displayed all over the garden, and forever cast in stone as a reminder to everyone that every work done with a labor of love and passion is a masterpiece – and probably deserves a statue!

Here are the details of this off – beaten path:

Location: 79, Rue de Varenne, 7th arrondissement
Contact No.: +33 1 44 18 61 10
Nearest Metro Station: Varenne

6. *Fondation Louis Vuitton*

The Fondation Louis Vuitton is located in Bois de Boulogne, and it is a fairly new contemporary art museum. It just opened to the public last October 2014. What's great about this museum is that tourists don't flock here for some reason; maybe it's because of the location which is why you should take advantage of going to this place because the moment you see it, your jaw will drop for sure! It contains contemporary art on the inside and it is literally made out of art on the outside. It's like the art came to life! What's most shocking about it is that it is not designed by a French artist; it is visualized by an American artist named Frank Gehry!

The interior of the building is just as complex as the exterior. The museum offers panoramic views from the different levels of the building as well.

The marvelous, and amazing architectural structure is truly revolutionary. It's a masterpiece, and it will literally beg you to gaze in awe of it. You don't actually need to come inside (but of course you still should) the building in itself is already a piece of magnificent art, one that will surely last and stand the test of time.

The place also holds various art exhibits, and events. You can bring your kids or loved ones with you because after gazing at this phenomenal structure, you can hang out and have fun with the rides at the Jardin d'Acclimatation nearby.

Here are the details of this off – beaten path:

Location: 8 Avenue du Mahatma Gandhi
Contact No.: +33 1 40 69 96 00
Nearest Metro Station: Les Sablons

7. *Saint – Chapelle*

For all the Catholics and religious people out there, if you wanted to have a soulful experience and truly connect with the Almighty without being distracted by tourists taking photos of the altar, then you should pray over at the Saint – Chappelle. This church is rich with history, and not a lot of tourists come here, even the Parisians themselves! Everyone is just magnetized by the spirit of the Notre Dame Cathedral or the Sacre Coeur Basilica. The Saint – Chappelle was exclusive only for French Kings back in the day. You can truly honor God just like all the French Kings that came before you!

The architectural interior structure of the church is just as beautiful as the Notre Dame; it is mostly made out of huge glass mosaics, and once the sun's light shines through it is illuminating the whole cathedral.

Another interesting fact is that since the church is situated in the middle of Paris' Court of Justice, you have to go through security check just like in an airport before entering the premises. So yes, you can find definitely find peace, solemnity, and (tight) security in this place religiously speaking, and literally speaking!

Here are the details of this off – beaten path:

Location: 6 Bd. du Palais, 1st arrondissement
Contact No.: Not Available
Nearest Metro Station: Cité

8. Musée Eugène Delacroix

At this point you might be sick of visiting different kinds of museums already, you might actually not even look at any kind of art once you get out of Paris, but let me give you one last recommendation before you dread this beautiful endeavor or genre forever.

Another off – the beaten place is called the Musée Eugène Delacroix. It is a little museum dedicated to also one of Paris' best - Eugène Delacroix. The place is his actual apartment, this is where he literally lived until his death in

1863. He painted his beautiful world – renowned canvass called the ---- in this very museum.

The location of it is also one of the most romantic places in Paris, it is unchartered territory by tourists, so if you are travelling with your significant other, this might be a good place appreciate beauty and intimacy. Most of Delacroix' work are still hanging on the walls of his apartment, you can wander around and truly experience what it's like to become an artist from his point of view.

The garden was renovated to make it look like what it is on his day. You might really pursue painting after experiencing the atmosphere in this place. You will get the real feeling of what it is like living as an artist!

Here are the details of this off – beaten path:

Location: 6, Rue de Furstenberg, 6th arrondissement
Contact No.: +33 1 44 41 86 50
Nearest Metro Station: St. Germain des Près

9. Passage Vivienne

Ever wondered what's it like living in Paris France in the 19th century? Well, wonder no more!
The post – revolution days of Paris still exist in Passage Vivienne! If you wanted to see the remnants of the post – revolution era, and experience how the middle – class lived, then check out this place.

The passage is of course out of sight for tourists, and locals, but it is just hiding in plain sight right behind another famous attraction, the Palais Royal. Try passage hopping in Paris especially during a rainy day! Get cozy and warm in some of its café bars and restaurants.

Here are the details of this off – beaten path:

Location: Rue des Petits Champs

Contact No.: N/A
Nearest Metro Station: Bourse

10. Cimetière du Père Lachaise

"There is only one God and his name is Death.
And there is only one thing we say to Death: Not today."

- George R.R. Martin (Game of Thrones)

You might be curious as to why a cemetery is included in this list. Well aside from the fact that the Cimetière du Père Lachaise is yet another work of art and the most visited necropolis in Paris, it is particularly included because this is where a lot of famous French artists are buried. It is perhaps a reminder; that even the greatest artists who ever lived will all face the same fate in the end – death.

The Père Lachaise cemetery takes its name from King Louis XIV's confessor, Father François d'Aix de La Chaise. It covers 44 hectares and contains over 70,000 burial plots (and counting). The funeral park also projects French art and gothic architecture through the designs of the graves, mausoleums, and burial chambers. The remains of various French artists and famous people lie in this cemetery including Edith Piaf, Frédéric Chopin, Honoré de Balzac, Guillaume Apollinaire, Yves Montand, Jean-François Champollion, Alfred de Musset, Camille Pissarro, Jim Morrison, Jean de La Fontaine, and Oscar Wilde.

The funeral park is very prestigious that there is even a guided tour of the cemetery, but since this is supposed to be an off – beaten path, it is highly recommended that you wander around the Cimetière du Père Lachaise by yourself, just so you can genuinely feel the place, and be able to appreciate life even more! It may be cliché but it's the truth - life is short. We're all going to die on our own time, and in our unique way, but for now let's learn to live, seize every moment and own every second of it.

Here are the details of this off – beaten path:

Location: 16 Rue du Repos

Contact No.: +33 1 55 25 82 10

Nearest Metro Station: Philippe-Auguste station

Quick Travel Guide

"The carrots are cooked" is a popular catchphrase in France. It simply means that it's a done deal. I hope you're dreams or plans of visiting the vivacious city of Paris are non – negotiable. Do everything you can to at least have a glimpse of this beautiful paradise. You won't regret it.

Give time and don't pass up this opportunity of a lifetime. You can never experience the fullness of its beauty until you get to see it with your own eyes.

What are you waiting for? I am sure that you are thrilled to explore Paris, but before this comes to an end, here is a quick travel guide. This contains the summary of all the places you've just read through as well as the necessary information that you need before traveling to Paris.
Bon Voyage!

1. *Paris Quick Facts*
    a. Currency – Euros (€)
    b. Primary Language spoken: French
    c. Weather and seasons - has a temperate climate with mild winters and summers.

- **Spring** - March 21 to June 21; the average temperature during spring is 10oC – 20oC.
- **Summer** – June 21 to September 21; Average temperature during summer is 23oC – 24oC.
- **Autumn** – September 21 to December 21; Average temperature during autumn is 15oC – 21oC.
- **Winter** - December 21 to March 21; the average temperature during winter is 2oC – 7oC.

2. *Transportation*

Transportation Services in Paris

- Airplane
- Paris Metro Train/ Regional Express Network
- Airport buses/ Noctilien buses
- Seine River Tour Cruise
- Trams
- Taxi *Parisien*

3. *Travel Essentials*

Immigration and Visas

- For tourists in general, you need to have Schengen Visa (valid only for 90 days or 3 months). If you are planning to stay in France for more than 3 months, (either for work purposes or personal matters) then you need to apply for a long-stay visa provided that you have presented appropriate documents needed or reasons for your longer stay.

Money Exchange

- The currency in France is called Euros. You may want to exchange your national money to any banks around Paris, or better yet to the exchange bureaus.

ATMs and Credit Cards

- ATMs are found almost everywhere and are available 24/7.
- Credit cards such as Visa and MasterCard are accepted in various hotels, restaurants, and shops. An American Express card may not be accepted everywhere.

Electric and Voltage

- Paris' standard electrical voltage is 230 volts or 50 Hz AC.

Communication Services

- There are four operators in France; the whole country is covered by GSM 900, 1800, GPRS, and HSPDA network. There are over 400 Wi-Fi hotspots around the city.

- Connect to 'Orange' network so that you can have free internet access.

Paris Highlights

1.) Where to Stay

Here's a quick list of the districts in Paris where you can stay during your trip.

- Le Marais District
- St. Germain - des - Pres District
- Montmartre District
- 9th District
- Ile Saint - Louis District
- Belleville District
- Opera District
- Champs - Elysées
- Gare de Lyon District
- Wagram Monceau

2.) Where to Eat

Here's a quick list of the food districts in Paris where you can eat.

- 11th Arrondissement
- *10th Arrondissement*

- *8th Arrondissement*
- *9th Arrondissement*
- *2nd Arrondissement*
- *6th Arrondissement*
- 3rd Arrondissement
- *1st Arrondissement*
- *18th Arrondissement*
- 4th Arrondissement

3.) Where to Shop

Here's a quick list of the shopping districts of Paris.

- Avenue des Champs Elysees
- Rue de Rennes
- Haussmann – Opera
- Rue de Rivoli - Le Marais
- Rue des Martyrs
- Rue Saint-Honoré
- Montmartre District
- Rue de Passy

- Avenue des Ternes
- Quartier Beaubourg et Les Halles

4.) Tourists Spots

Here's a quick list of the famous tourist destinations in Paris.

- The Eiffel Tower
- Louvre Museum and Pyramid
- Notre Dame Cathedral (Notre Dame de Paris)
- Seine River
- Sacré Coeur Basilica
- Château de Versailles (Palace of Versailles)
- Pantheon
- L'Hotel National des Invalides
- Élysée Palace
- Arc de Triomphe

5.) Interacting with Paris

Here's a quick list of the interesting things you can do while in Paris.

- Opéra National de Paris - Palais Garnier

- Moulin Rouge Theater
- Musée d'Art moderne de la Ville de Paris
- Jardin des Tuileries
- Maison européenne de la photographie
- Centre de Création Artistique
- Grand Musée du Parfum
- Parc zoologique de Thoiry
- Cité de l'Architecture & du Patrimoine
- Jardin du Luxembourg

6.) Nightlife in Paris

Here's a quick list of the places you can hang out at night in Paris.

- Bastille
- Oberkampf
- Ménilmontant and Gambetta
- The Marais
- Belleville
- Champs-Elysées
- Montmartre and Pigalle

- Grands Boulevards and Sentier
- St – Germain – des – Prés
- Place Vendome - Faubourg St-Honoré

7.) Off – Beaten Path in Paris

Here's a quick list of the unchartered territories you can explore in Paris.

- Gaîté Lyrique
- *La Pagode*
- *Le Ballon de Paris*
- Le Carreau du Temple
- Musée Rodin
- *Fondation Louis Vuitton*
- *Saint – Chapelle*
- Musée Eugène Delacroix
- Passage Vivienne
- Cimetière du Père Lachaise

PHOTO REFERENCES

Page 1 Photo Walkerssk by via Pixabay,

https://pixabay.com/en/paris-france-eiffel-tower-night-1836415

Page 5 Photo by tpsdave via Pixabay,

https://pixabay.com/en/paris-france-city-urban-sky-1804483

Page 6 Photo by Pline via Wikimedia Commons,

https://commons.wikimedia.org/wiki/Paris#/media/File:Toit-Grand-Palais.jpg

Page 12 Photo by PhOtOnQuAnTiQuE via Flickr,

https://www.flickr.com/photos/photonquantique/6115462673

Page 16 Photo by Christian Bélanger via Flickr

<https://www.flickr.com/photos/krissserz/14297584148/in/photolist-nMqRDw>

Page 17 Photo by J Aaron Farr via Flickr

<https://www.flickr.com/photos/jaaronfarr/519948326/>

Page 33 Photo by EdiNugraha via Pixabay,

https://pixabay.com/en/paris-the-arc-de-triomphe-monument-102843

Page 40 Photo by Unsplash via Pixabay,

https://pixabay.com/en/building-hotel-classic-architecture-768505/

Page 42 Photo by GothPhil via Flickr,

https://www.flickr.com/photos/phil_p/4999201317/

Page 44 Photo by Roman Boed via Flickr,

https://www.flickr.com/photos/romanboed/15300724715/

Page 46 Photo by Allan Watt via Flickr,

https://www.flickr.com/photos/130467353@N06/16436404262

Page 48 Photo by David McKelvey via Flickr,

https://www.flickr.com/photos/dgmckelvey/9283019089/

Page 50 Photo by JR P via Flickr,

https://www.flickr.com/photos/ugardener/29658825610/

Page 52 Photo by Groume via Flickr,

https://www.flickr.com/photos/groume/4728948884/

Page 54 Photo by Rodrigo Soldon via Flickr,

https://www.flickr.com/photos/soldon/5477472457/

Page 56 Photo by Jonathan via Flickr,

https://www.flickr.com/photos/iceninejon/16225754150/

Page 58 Photo by AlNo via Wikimedia Commons,

https://commons.wikimedia.org/wiki/File:Paris_GareDeLyon_FacadeEtTourDeLHorloge.JPG

Page 60 Photo by Tom Sowerby via Flickr,

https://www.flickr.com/photos/tomsowerby/4730921814/

Page 62 Photo by skeeze via Pixabay,

https://pixabay.com/en/wine-cheese-bread-caf%C3%A9-paris-905098/

Page 63 Photo by TomEats via Flickr,

https://www.flickr.com/photos/walsh02/4636745644/in/photostream/

Page 65 Photo by Meg Zimbeck via Flickr,

https://www.flickr.com/photos/mufoo/2188904817/

Page 67 Photo by Clement Lo via Flickr,

https://www.flickr.com/photos/alacuisine/1444744649/

Page 69 Photo by Phil Beard via Flickr,

https://www.flickr.com/photos/8592508@N04/4945053771/

Page 71 Photo by Corinne Moncelli via Flickr,

https://www.flickr.com/photos/hotels-paris-rive-gauche/3950181198/

Page 73 Photo by Jeremy Keith via Flickr,

https://www.flickr.com/photos/adactio/499637694/in/photolist

Page 75 Photo by Connie Ma via Flickr,

https://www.flickr.com/photos/ironypoisoning/14321436730/

Page 77 Photo by Guilhem Vellut via Flickr,

https://www.flickr.com/photos/o_0/27667637582/

Page 78 Photo by Philippe blayo photography via Flickr,

https://www.flickr.com/photos/papacamera/4693307359/

Page 80 Photo by Andrea Schaffer via Flickr,

https://www.flickr.com/photos/aschaf/4947566073/

Page 82 Photo by skeeze via Pixabay,

https://pixabay.com/en/printemps-department-store-exterior-535685/

Page 83 Photo by Abir Anwar via Flickr,

https://www.flickr.com/photos/abir82/468331344/

Page 86 Photo by Patrick Nouhailler via Flickr,

https://www.flickr.com/photos/patrick_nouhailler/7549450340/

Page 88 Photo by Roberto Ventre via Flickr,

https://www.flickr.com/photos/robie06/3594181839/

Page 90 Photo by lereile lereile via Flickr,

https://www.flickr.com/photos/lereile/378634234/

Page 92 Photo by Mariano Mantel via Flickr,

https://www.flickr.com/photos/mariano-mantel/8192176790/

Page 94 Photo by Rose Trinh via Flickr,

https://www.flickr.com/photos/rosebennet/5209607260/

Page 96 Photo by Henrik Berger Jørgensen via Flickr,

https://www.flickr.com/photos/darkb4dawn/3299324334/

Page 98 Photo by Rama via Wikimedia Commons,

https://commons.wikimedia.org/wiki/File:Rue-de-paris-film97jpg.jpg

Page 100 Photo by Patrick janicek via Flickr,

https://www.flickr.com/photos/marsupilami92/5754537951/

Page 102 Photo by Maxi via Flickr,

https://www.flickr.com/photos/57276764@N00/2511901487/

Page 105 Photo by Fred Po via Flickr,

https://www.flickr.com/photos/aline-et-fred/27005281500/

Page 106 Photo by Y Nakanishi via Flickr,

https://www.flickr.com/photos/ynakanishi/31983607703/

Page 109 Photo by EdiNugraha via Pixabay,

https://pixabay.com/en/louvre-pyramid-paris-architecture-102840/

Page 112 Photo by Anna & Michal via Flickr,

https://www.flickr.com/photos/michalo/6094164096/

Page 115 Photo by brian_ytsu via Flickr,

https://www.flickr.com/photos/principle/14143379125/

Page 118 Photo by skeeze via Pixabay,

https://pixabay.com/en/seine-river-sunset-paris-city-905055/

Page 121 Photo by cthkim via Pixabay,

https://pixabay.com/en/montmartre-chakra-kweeo-paris-1607576/

Page 124 Photo by Roland Turner via Flickr,

https://www.flickr.com/photos/sisaphus/4485467946/

Page 127 Photo by Nick Loyless via Flickr,

https://www.flickr.com/photos/nloyless/9381431686/

Page 130 Photo by Steve Hanna via Flickr,

https://www.flickr.com/photos/justonlysteve/4795064438/

Page 133 Photo by Nicolas Nova via Flickr,

https://www.flickr.com/photos/nnova/8928226199/

Page 137 Photo by Benjamin Stäudinger via Flickr,

https://www.flickr.com/photos/ontourwithben/7697123086/

Page 138 Photo by Javier via Flickr,

https://www.flickr.com/photos/javisitges/7424509016/

Page 141 Photo by Fougerouse Arnaud via Flickr,

https://www.flickr.com/photos/hihaa/12862109645/

Page 143 Photo by skeeze via Pixabay,

https://pixabay.com/en/moulin-rouge-paris-red-mill-1050325/

Page 145 Photo by Mark B. Schlemmer via Flickr,

https://www.flickr.com/photos/mbschlemmer/6176785732/

Page 148 Photo by Florian via Flickr,

https://www.flickr.com/photos/florian_the_great/5319056167

Page 151 Photo by cyberien 94 via Flickr,

https://www.flickr.com/photos/philemon94/6448947523/

Page 153 Photo by via Guilhem Vellut Wikimedia Commons,

https://commons.wikimedia.org/wiki/File:Cent_Quatre_@_Paris_(28546460652).jpg

Page 156 Photo by Nico Paix via Flickr,

https://www.flickr.com/photos/aerosolhalos/4766462508/

Page 158 Photo by Philippe Berdalle via Flickr,

https://www.flickr.com/photos/berdcris2011/364895052/

Page 160 Photo by via stephane333 Wikimedia Commons,

https://commons.wikimedia.org/wiki/File:Paris_juin_2010_Maison_Europ%C3%A9enne_de_la_Photographie.jpg

Page 163 Photo by Corine Moncelli via Flickr,

https://www.flickr.com/photos/hotels-paris-rive-gauche/2170882099/in/photostream/

Page 164 Photo by Miriamichelle via Pixabay,

https://pixabay.com/en/paris-france-landmark-sky-clouds-341086/

Page 166 Photo by superUbO via Flickr,

https://www.flickr.com/photos/superubo/5609318520/

Page 168 Photo by Dukas Ju via Flickr,

https://www.flickr.com/photos/59558222@N06/8215153594/

Page 170 Photo by Ali Catterall via Flickr,

https://www.flickr.com/photos/45375656@N00/4204710872/

Page 172 Photo by carolus124 via Flickr,

https://www.flickr.com/photos/cafes-paris/1947577837/

Page 174 Photo by Martha Heinemann Bixby via Flickr,

https://www.flickr.com/photos/mjhbixby6/5655079893/

Page 176 Photo by Guilhem Vellut via Wikimedia Commons,

https://commons.wikimedia.org/wiki/File:Belleville_@_Paris_(29418764246).jpg

Page 178 Photo by Yann Forget via Wikimedia Commons,

https://commons.wikimedia.org/wiki/File:Avenue_des_Champs-%C3%89lys%C3%A9es_at_night,_Paris.jpg

Page 180 Photo by Thomas sauzedde via Flickr,

https://www.flickr.com/photos/idirectori/6107651916/

Page 182 Photo by Marc Ben Fatma via Flickr,

https://www.flickr.com/photos/benymarc/4916026274/

Page 185 Photo by Francesco Dazzi via Flickr,

https://www.flickr.com/photos/checco/2862479787/

Page 186 Photo by Luc Mercelis via Flickr,

https://www.flickr.com/photos/luc-mechelen/26842492394/

Page 188 Photo by Chris Goldberg via Flickr,

https://www.flickr.com/photos/chrisgold/7398790756/

Page 190 Photo by Laurent Neyssensas via Flickr,

https://www.flickr.com/photos/loneyss/9757882041/

Page 192 Photo by David Monniaux via Wikimedia Commons,

https://commons.wikimedia.org/wiki/File:Bois_de_Vincennes_DSC03761.JPG

Page 194 Photo by LisArt via Flickr,

https://www.flickr.com/photos/lisartdesign/7336168334/

Page 196 Photo by besopha via Wikimedia Commons,

https://commons.wikimedia.org/wiki/File:Carreau_du_Temple,_Paris_2015.jpg

Page 198 Photo by Tammy Lo via Wikimedia Commons,

https://commons.wikimedia.org/wiki/File:The_Thinker,_Mus%C3%A9e_Rodin,_Paris_September_2013_003.jpg

Page 200 Photo by Jacqueline Poggi via Flickr,

https://www.flickr.com/photos/jacqueline_poggi/1541974291
4/

Page 202 Photo by Randi Hausken via Flickr,

https://www.flickr.com/photos/randihausken/2862673181/

Page 204 Photo by Storm Crypt via Flickr,

https://www.flickr.com/photos/storm-crypt/3790548505/

Page 205 Photo by Lionel Allorge via Wikimedia Commons,

https://commons.wikimedia.org/wiki/File:Paris_Galerie_Vivi
enne_2012_17.jpg

Page 207 Photo by Malinche via Flickr,

https://www.flickr.com/photos/malinche/92458796/

REFERENCES

"5 Incredible Facts about the Paris Opera House" Random Acts of Kelliness http://www.randomactsofkelliness.com/5-incredible-facts-paris-opera-house/

"5 reasons why Paris is the City of Love" My Austrian Blog http://www.myaustrianblog.at/en/2014/02/5-reasons-why-paris-is-the-city-of-love/

"7 Interesting Facts about Paris' Moulin Rouge" Customized Tips https://customizedtips.wordpress.com/2014/06/02/7 interesting-facts-about-paris-moulin-rouge/

"A bit of trivia about Paris' Opera Garnier" Paris Pass http://blog.parispass.com/trivia-about-paris-opera-garnier/#.WLpuENJ97Dd

"A Culinary Guide to the 20 Arrondissements in Paris" Eater http://www.eater.com/2016/10/19/13324216/paris-guide-arrondissements-neighborhoods

"All the Paris Arrondissements, Ranked By Their Food & Drink" Thrillist https://www.thrillist.com/eat/paris/paris-arrondissements-ranked-by-their-food-and-drink

"Cimetière du Père Lachaise" ParisTourism http://en.parisinfo.com/paris-museum-monument/71470/Cimeti%C3%A8re-du-P%C3%A8re-Lachaise

"Cité de l'architecture & du patrimoine" Paris Tourism http://en.parisinfo.com/paris-museum-monument/71083/Cite-de-l-architecture-du-patrimoine

"Contemporary Art in Paris" Paris Tourism http://en.parisinfo.com/what-to-see-in-paris/contemporary-art-in-paris

"Facts About The Pantheon In Paris" Pantheon Paris http://www.pantheonparis.com/history/facts

"Five Fascinating But Little-Known Museums of Photograph in Paris" Paris Insider's Guide http://www.parisinsidersguide.com/paris-museums-photography.html

"Fondation Louis Vuitton" Paris Tourism http://en.parisinfo.com/paris-museum-monument/71286/Fondation-Louis-Vuitton

"Getting a tourist visa for France" Come to Paris http://www.cometoparis.com/paris-guide/france-travel-information/getting-a-tourist-visa-for-france

"Grand Musée du Parfum" Paris Tourism http://en.parisinfo.com/what-to-see-in-paris/info/guides/grand-musee-du-parfum-paris

"How to get to and around Paris" Paris Tourism http://en.parisinfo.com/practical-paris/how-to-get-to-and-around-paris

"Jardin du Luxembourg" Paris Tourism http://en.parisinfo.com/paris-museum-monument/71393/Jardin-du-Luxembourg

"Jardin des Tuileries Beautiful French style garden" Parisianist https://www.parisianist.com/en/attractions/parks-and-gardens/jardin-des-tuileries

"Les Invalides" Earth in Pictures http://www.earthinpictures.com/world/france/paris/les_invalides.html

"Modern and contemporary art museums" Paris Tourism http://en.parisinfo.com/what-to-see-in-paris/contemporary-art-in-paris/contemporary-art-hotspots/modern-and-contemporary-art-museums

"Musee d'Art Moderne de la Ville de Paris" Wanderbat http://museums.wanderbat.com/l/761/Musee-d-Art-Moderne-de-la-Ville-de-Paris

"Nightlife in Paris: 10 Best Districts to Hit for a Night Out" Go Paris http://goparis.about.com/od/nightlifeinparis/ss/Nightlife-in-Paris-10-Best-Districts-to-Hit-For-a-Night-Out.htm#step11

"Notre-Dame: Facts About the Cathedral in Paris" Primary Facts http://primaryfacts.com/2699/notre-dame-facts-about-the-cathedral-in-paris/

"Off the beaten track: 12 secret spots in Paris" Momondo https://www.momondo.com/inspiration/12-things-to-see-in-paris/#wz5T5I2bjWOCPgQk.97

"Parc zoologique de Thoiry" Paris Tourism
http://en.parisinfo.com/paris-museum-monument/72776/Parc-zoologique-de-Thoiry

"Paris" Wikipedia
https://en.wikipedia.org/wiki/Paris

"Paris Hotels: Where to Stay in Paris" Hotel Grand Paris
http://www.hotelsgrandparis.com/quartiers-paris-arrondissement.html

"Top 5 Fun Facts About Montmartre" Discover Walks
https://www.discoverwalks.com/blog/top-5-fun-facts-about-montmartre/

"The 10 Best Shopping Streets in Paris" Paris Is Paris
http://parisisparis.com/shopping/the-10-best-shopping-streets-in-paris/

"Top 10 Facts about the Sacré-Cœur, Paris" French Moments
https://frenchmoments.eu/top-10-facts-about-the-sacre-coeur-paris/

"Top 10 Unusual Things to Do in Paris" The Culture Trip https://theculturetrip.com/europe/france/paris/articles/off-the-beaten-track-top-10-unusual-things-to-do-in-paris/

"The Centre Pompidou, Centre of Art and Culture" Paris Tourism
http://en.parisinfo.com/what-to-do-in-paris/info/guides/exhibition-at-the-centre-pompidou

"The Main Paris Tourist Attractions" About - France
http://about-france.com/paris-tourist-attractions.htm

"The newly opened Le Grand Musée du Parfum in Paris Tells the Story of Fragrance" The National
http://www.thenational.ae/arts-life/art/the-newly-opened-le-grand-muse-du-parfum-in-paris-tells-the-story-of-fragrance

"Useful info" Paris Tourism
http://en.parisinfo.com/practical-paris/useful-info

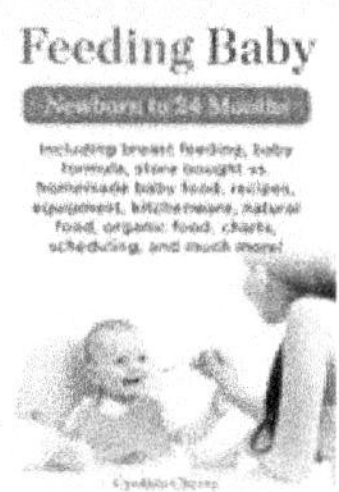

Feeding Baby
Cynthia Cherry
978-1941070000

Axolotl
Lolly Brown
978-0989658430

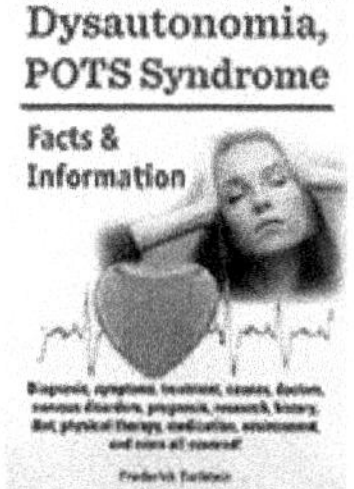

Dysautonomia, POTS Syndrome
Frederick Earlstein
978-0989658485

Degenerative Disc Disease Explained
Frederick Earlstein
978-0989658485

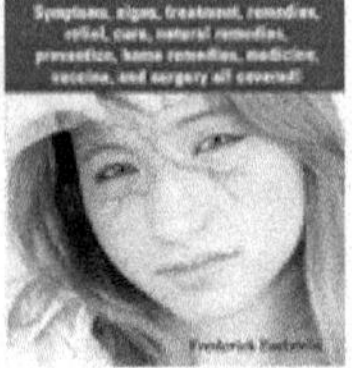

Sinusitis, Hay Fever,
Allergic Rhinitis Explained
Frederick Earlstein
978-1941070024

Wicca
Riley Star
978-1941070130

Zombie Apocalypse
Rex Cutty
978-1941070154

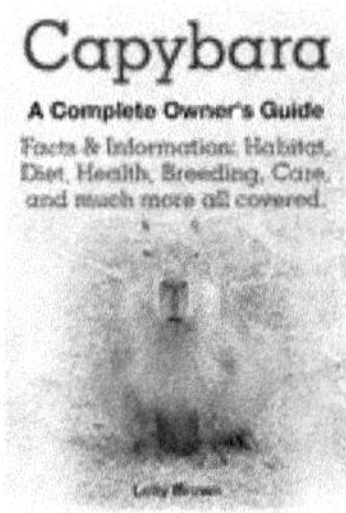

Capybara
Lolly Brown
978-1941070062

Eels As Pets
Lolly Brown
978-1941070167

Scabies and Lice Explained
Frederick Earlstein
978-1941070017

Saltwater Fish As Pets
Lolly Brown
978-0989658461

Torticollis Explained
Frederick Earlstein
978-1941070055

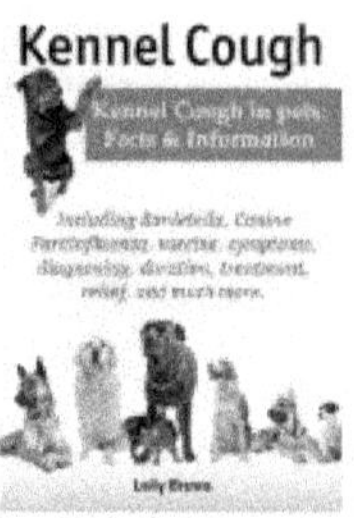

Kennel Cough
Lolly Brown
978-0989658409

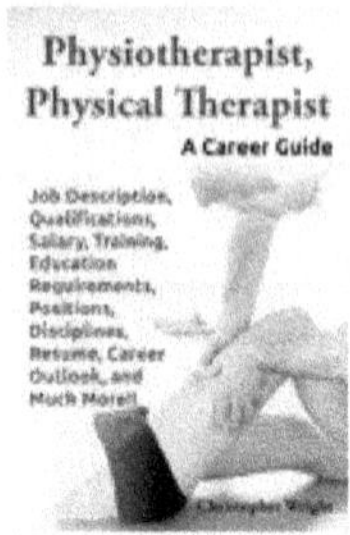

Physiotherapist, Physical Therapist
Christopher Wright
978-0989658492

Rats, Mice, and Dormice As Pets
Lolly Brown
978-1941070079

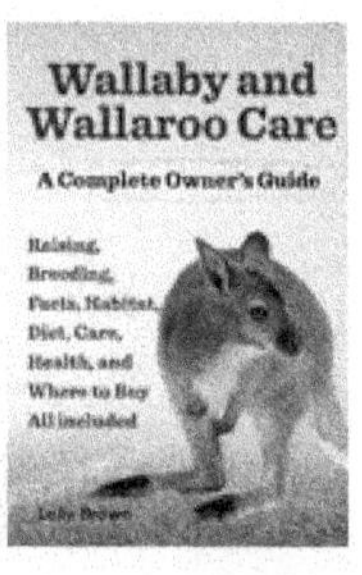

Wallaby and Wallaroo Care
Lolly Brown
978-1941070031

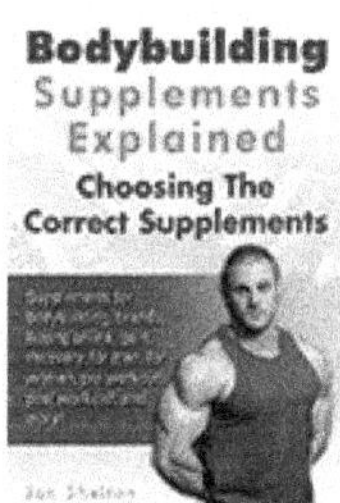

Bodybuilding Supplements
Explained
Jon Shelton
978-1941070239

Demonology
Riley Star
978-19401070314

Pigeon Racing
Lolly Brown
978-1941070307

Dwarf Hamster
Lolly Brown
978-1941070390

Cryptozoology
Rex Cutty
978-1941070406

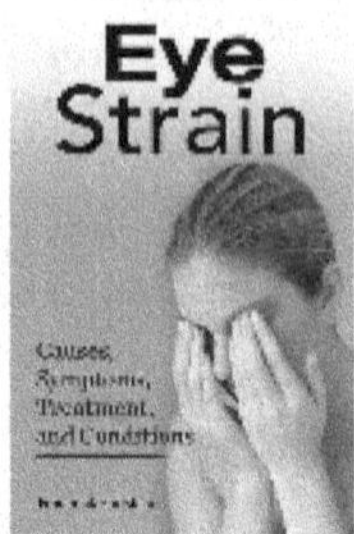

Eye Strain
Frederick Earlstein
978-1941070369

Inez The Miniature Elephant
Asher Ray
978-1941070353

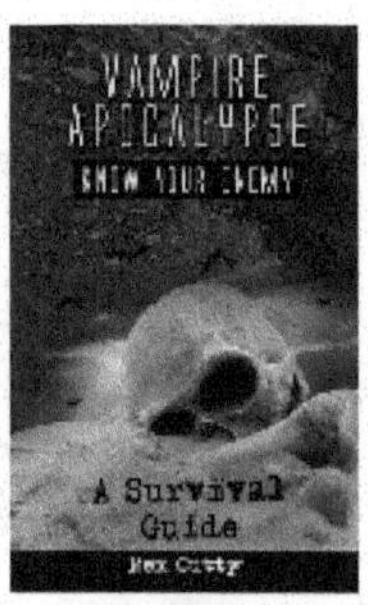

Vampire Apocalypse
Rex Cutty
978-1941070321

www.ingramcontent.com/pod-product-compliance
Lightning Source LLC
Chambersburg PA
CBHW051950090426
42741CB00008B/1342

* 9 7 8 1 9 4 6 2 8 6 1 6 1 *